GOOD CHRISTIANS BREAK BAD LAWS

OBEYING GOD IN A FALLEN WORLD

GOOD CHRISTIANS BREAK BAD LAWS,
WRITTEN BY TOPHER FIELD, © 2024

COVER DESIGN BY CARLY SODERSTROM,
GOOD CHRISTIANS BREAK BAD LAWS TYPOGRAPHIC DESIGN BY CARLY SODERSTROM.

PRINTED BY AMAZON

PUBLISHER CONTACT: publish@lockepress.com

AUTHOR CONTACT: topher@topherfield.net

ISBN: 978-0-6455161-9-7

GOOD CHRISTIANS BREAK BAD LAWS

OBEYING GOD IN A FALLEN WORLD

TOPHER FIELD

Table of Contents

Foreword:
Concerning 'Good Christians'

If you listen to popular culture you'll believe that when someone says "I'm a Christian" what they're really saying is "I'm better than you" or "God loves me more," but if you understand your Bible then you understand that nothing could be further from the truth.

"I'm a Christian," when properly understood from the Bible, is an admission that I'm *not* better than you *and* that I know it!

"I'm a Christian" means I'm completely unworthy of forgiveness for my great sins and powerless to overcome them by my own 'goodness'… but I'm forgiven by the grace of God alone and *not* because of anything I did to earn forgiveness.

To give a fuller explanation, "I'm a Christian" means "I was a wretched sinner, beyond hope of salvation, and even my best efforts, my greatest works, my most 'perfect' moments were like filthy rags compared to the perfection of God. In my own strength I could *never* earn salvation and I'd be condemned to Hell forever—*and I deserve Hell* because of my sin. But God, in His mercy, made a way through the death and resurrection of Jesus Christ (who was God in human form, the only sinless man who ever lived) so that He paid the price of my sin by enduring a physical death more torturous and painful than any other. He went to Hell, did battle with the fallen angel Satan, conquered sin and death, and rose again after three days, and has now ascended into Heaven and is seated on the right hand of God the Father where He intercedes for me. Because of Him, I have been adopted into God's family by grace through faith, my sins are forgiven, my record has been wiped, I share in the victory and authority of Christ, I am seated with Christ at the right hand of our father God, and I will spend eternity in Heaven *as though I had never sinned...* and you can too!"

That is what "I'm a Christian" means.

But many people don't realise this truth, so when someone says "I'm a Christian" someone will quickly object: "You can't be a Christian, because you did X!" where 'X' is some sin or other, some hypocrisy, some weakness that, in the minds of those who do not understand what "I'm a Christian" means, means you're not a Christian!

"I'm a Christian" is not a claim to perfection. It doesn't mean "I've got my life together," or that you must always be positive, organised, successful, healthy, in a perfect marriage and family, or never have a bad day.

You (and I) are flawed, sinful, at times hypocritical, and rarely able to spend so much as one full day truly living up to the ideal of Christlikeness that we aspire to.

That's absolutely true.

I grew up as a pastor's kid and I can attest to the pressure to 'perform,' to 'look like a Christian' and worse, to 'look like a pastor's kid.' On more than one occasion my father had the 'your behaviour reflects on me' conversation with me because I'd been foolish or childish or some similar thing. He meant well, but the message I heard was, "Put on a face," "Pretend to be better," "Hide the ugly truth."

And so, like many Christians who are broken (which is *all* of us), I did exactly that. I still believed in God, but my life split in two and though I looked good on the outside, on the inside was a shallow performance based version of Christianity.

I wish I could be like Paul and say "Emulate me even as I emulate Christ," but I can't. For many years the reality of my life has not been at all like a Christian.

A 'good Christian' is a *bad* person whose sins are forgiven and who, in response to their salvation (not to be confused with 'working for' salvation) has dedicated themself to 'doing good' as we are exhorted by Paul, Peter, and Jesus to do.

We know that by ourselves "There is none good, no, not one," that our "heart is deceitful and desperately wicked," and that we have nothing 'good' to offer to God: "all our righteousness is like filthy rags", and any 'good' we do is only by the power of Christ working in us [Psalm 14:3; Jeremiah 17:9; Isiah 64:6].

But we *also* know that in Christ we have new life, our heart is made new and circumcised to God, our sins are forgiven by the sacrifice of Jesus, we can be washed by the water of the word, and we have victory in our new life as new creations in Christ Jesus [Romans 8].

So my title, '*Good Christians Break Bad Laws*' is not a claim that I or anyone else deserves the title of 'good' in our *own* strength. Not at all. It points instead to the reality that as we 'run the race' we seek to *do* good in *response* to our salvation, as an act of love and voluntary service to God.

This book is about the fact that sometimes it will not be possible to *do* good before God *and* obey the laws of men.

It's an acknowledgement that at times it is not possible to obey both God *and* man and in those moments we must choose to do good with a clear conscience before God and accept the consequences from the law of man.

I'm done trying to be 'good' in my own strength and you should be too. Today my walk with God is the most intimate, honest, and real that it's ever been, and I can tell you with absolute honesty that it's sometimes a walk, sometimes a crawl, and often a stumble and fall, but God's mercies are new every morning and so I walk with Him daily. As King David tells us in the Psalms, God remembers that we are but flesh [Psalm 78:39; Psalm 103:14]. He knows our every weakness and He chose to make a way of salvation *despite* who we are, not because of who we are [Ephesians 2:8-9].

By God's grace I aim to live out my days on this earth in faithful service to Him and then to enter His presence for eternity and be welcomed with the words, "Well done, my good and faithful servant," and then enjoy an eternal reward that I *do not deserve*, no matter how many 'good' works I may do. It's a reward which was bought for me by the sacrifice made by Jesus Christ and given to me freely as a gift by grace through faith.

I hope I see you there in Heaven too, enjoying a reward that *you* don't deserve either.

But while we are still here on this earth let us dedicate ourselves to obeying God and *doing good* even, indeed *especially*, when our government goes bad.

A Time to Choose

"Choose you this day whom you will serve." — Joshua 24:15

Joshua stood in front of the Children of Israel and gave them the clearest possible ultimatum.

The time for compromise was over.

Their ancestors had a long history of abandoning God and turning back to idols the moment the going got tough, or paradoxically, when things got too good. Even in the face of incredible miracles such as the parting of the Red Sea, manna from Heaven, the pillar of fire and cloud and more, it seemed the Israelites were never more than mere moments away from falling back into unbelief and idolatry.

Only Joshua and Caleb were left from the older, rebellious generation, which had first reached the edge of the Promised Land more than forty years earlier.

That entire generation had since died in the wilderness because of their unbelief. Only Caleb and Joshua had faith that God would deliver that fertile and prosperous land out of the hands of the giants who lived there and into to the hands of Israel. So God judged them with forty extra years in the wilderness and of the people over twenty years of age only Joshua and Caleb survived to enter Canaan [Numbers 14:30].

Joshua and Caleb had witnessed firsthand how quickly their ancestors had turned away from God on the painful journey from Egypt to Canaan, and Joshua knew that this moment was a dangerous one.

The children of Israel had conquered the Promised Land at last after generations of captivity, decades of wilderness, and years of war.

This generation had conquered where their ancestors had failed, but would they now remain true to the God that had given them the victory? Or would they turn away in the good times as their ancestors had time and again?

They had won battles against the Canaanites, but would they win the war against their own idolatry and remain faithful to the God who had given them this land of milk and honey?

Would they remain faithful to the Giver, now that they had the gift?

And so, before he formally ended the campaign of conquest and allowed the people of the new nation of Israel to go to their newly conquered homes and enjoy the rest promised by God some 450 years earlier, Joshua laid out their next challenge in the clearest possible terms:

[God] gave you a land where you had not laboured, and cities which you built not, but you dwell therein; of vineyards and oliveyards which you planted not, but you do eat.

Now therefore fear Jehovah, and serve him in sincerity and in truth; and put away the gods which your fathers served beyond the River, and in Egypt; and serve Jehovah.

And if it seem evil unto you to serve Jehovah, ***choose you this day whom ye will serve****; whether the gods which your fathers served that were beyond the River, or the gods of the Amorites, in whose land ye dwell: but as for me and my house, we will serve Jehovah.*

And the people answered and said, Far be it from us that we should forsake Jehovah, to serve other gods.

— Joshua 24:13-16

The rest, of course, is history. Throughout the books of Chronicles, Kings, Judges, and the prophets, time and again—even *after* they received the gift of the Promised Land from God—the children of Israel turned back to idols and abandoned the one true God.

And time and again God brought them back to worshipping Him, usually by bringing some sort of trial and hardship, including allowing them to be conquered and dragged away into captivity, until they cried out to God and He would rescue them again.

But this is just ancient history right? We don't have idols today, do we? Sure, we might refer to sports stars as 'idols' and have a TV show called 'American Idol,' but that's just a turn of phrase... we're not building golden calves and worshipping the works of our own hands and placing our faith in a false God... are we?

I remember that when I learned the Ten Commandments in Sunday school, "Thou shalt have no other gods before me" seemed an out-dated and completely unnecessary commandment in the modern world!

Surely the worship of idols was just a relic of history? No one in the *modern* world would be so silly as to worship a god they made with their own hands... would they?

Over the course of this book I will endeavour to convince you that today *everything* is different... and yet somehow it is also *exactly* the same.

Throughout the world today we have most certainly built an idol—one that we worship and make sacrifices to in every way, and one that we place our faith in to meet all our needs—an idol that we trust in to replace God in the most literal ways possible.

Today's idol is made with human hands, although you can't see it like you can see a golden calf. Today's idol is something we pray to and make offerings and oaths to. Some people sacrifice the lives of others, or even their own lives, in service and worship of it.

Today's idol is Government.

The worship of government is *nothing* like the ancient worship of a golden calf... and yet it's *exactly* the same.

And, just as with the idols of old, we must choose who we will serve: the idol we made with our own hands, or the God who gave us hands in the first place. Because it's simply not possible to serve both God and government. The *government* is making sure of it.

As a Christian it's tempting to want to believe that we can be faithful to God and be good law-abiding citizens at the same time, and it's true that that *can* be possible... if the laws you live under are godly.

But it's no longer possible right now, because our laws are no longer godly, and it's the government that has deliberately made it impossible to obey both the government and God.

Around the world we're seeing governments step fully and finally into the place of God in every way. In the last few years we've seen governments reaching into the deepest and most private places of your life, including your faith, your prayers, your witness and service, and your created design and identity in God.

In this book I aim to give you insight into just what is going on, who is behind it, and what we as Christians ought to do about it.

This transformation of government from being a servant, to a master or indeed a god, has happened incrementally, and like the proverbial boiling frog most people are unaware.

Sadly it's inevitable that every man-made government will tread this path of idolatry, and it is difficult and costly to slow or reverse that 'progress.'

This is because of the spiritual forces at work in our world, and their love of power. The 'gods' of the ancient world have not gone away, they've rebranded, and in the modern world they use the mechanism of government and the mask of 'compassion' to advance their self-serving ambitions.

The basic pathway is, as the saying goes, "First they (people who rebel against God) demand tolerance, then acceptance, then celebration, and finally they make criminals of anyone who disagrees." This is the pathway of man's rebellion against God's design, and because governments are made by man this is how government aids and abets man's rebellion against God's created order.

This is currently most obvious in the mania around gender identity and transition. But while transgenderism is the current mania, it's not the first time we've seen the law being used to *deliberately* make it impossible to serve God *and* to be a law-abiding citizen at the same time.

I'll be arguing in this book that the exact same thing happened during Covid, that the same is happening with parenting and raising children, the same is happening with free speech, and in many other ways also.

Throughout this book I'll be using a lot of examples from Scripture, from history, and from my former home state of Victoria, Australia.

Many of the examples I will offer will be from the Covid madness as my home city of Melbourne, Australia, became the most locked-down city on earth. But I believe you'll recognise that the principle of what I'm saying applies in your own home too.

Given this global reality, we *must* have a discussion about what to do about it as Christians. In short, we *must* recognise that it's a time to choose.

If I'm right, and governments are intentionally becoming idols by making it impossible to serve God *and* obey them, then we really must discuss what that means, what the Bible says, whether civil disobedience has a place in Christian theology, and what the limits and parameters around that Christian civil disobedience are.

We must talk about the theology of civil disobedience.

This means far more than just a glib glance at Romans 13 or 1 Peter 2. It means a deep dive into the whole counsel of Scripture to understand our obligations as Christians who seek first and foremost to serve and honour God, in a world that is seemingly determined to make obedience to God a crime.

It is now a matter of urgency for us to decide:

Who will you serve, and how will you obey God in this fallen world?

God's Design for Government

Let us start at the very beginning, with God's original design for civil government.

The very first form of governance was the family, but in time God recognised this was no longer sufficient by itself (although it remains very crucial and God never intended to diminish the primacy of the family), and the first record we have of a God-ordained government was the system we know as 'Judges' in the Old Testament.

The initial concept is found in Exodus when Moses' father-in-law, Jethro, sees that it's impossible for Moses to keep up with the demand of judging all the disputes among the people of Israel [Exodus 18]. Jethro suggested appointing judges and leaders among the people so that only the most important or difficult cases would take Moses' time and all lesser cases would be judged by lesser judges.

God appears to have given tacit approval to this solution at the time, and the formalised system of Judges which we see later in the Bible is an evolution of this concept.

This was God's design, on purpose.

When God instituted government among the children of Israel He had a completely blank slate to work with. He could have written *any* system of government. The Israelites were a relatively sophisticated people with near universal reading, writing, and numeracy skills among males thirteen years and over, and relatively advanced metal, stone, wood, and cloth technologies. These were no primitive simpletons, and they had the capacity for social organisation to implement whatever form of government God prescribed.

God could have prescribed a monarchy, an oligarchy, a socialist 'paradise,' or some other concept beyond the capacity of our mortal minds to dream up... *all* options were on the table and God had the ability to communicate His choice to His people through Moses, Joshua, or any of the future prophets at any time.

So, what form of government did God prescribe? Nothing less than the most extremely small, low cost, efficient, and minimalist form of government in human history: judges.

Essentially, God wrote enough laws that an adult could read them in a few days, and designed a system of judges to arbitrate disputes... and that was it!

Notice that there was no mechanism to write more laws.

The only 'government' *per se* was a mechanism to resolve disputes about whether someone had broken the existing law or wronged another person.

This is what the judges were for, to arbitrate disputes, but there was no mechanism to make more laws.

Not only did God believe that the laws He had written were all that was needed, He also believed those were all the laws that would *ever* be needed!

It's difficult to imagine how a nation of more than one million inhabitants, with complex trade relationships, advanced (for the time) manufacturing, land ownership, and a thriving private sector could possibly operate with so few laws.

Today we have over 40,000 laws just in Australia. The number is no better in other Western democracies.

40,000 laws. Imagine trying to read them, much less understand them all!

And then, to really understand those 40,000 laws, you'd need to study all the court precedents and decisions that interpret those laws. Then you'd have to read, know, and understand the myriad bureaucratic rules and regulations from every government agency which govern every aspect of your life and you'd have to correctly parse their meanings, relationships, contradictions, and demands. And finally, you'd have to keep up as new laws, new regulations, and new court decisions are handed down.

Apologies for repeating a point that I also made in my first best-selling book, *Good People Break Bad Laws*, but we need to pause for a moment to consider the implications of a legal system like ours—a system where it's impossible to know the laws you're obligated to obey, paired with a 'justice' system that will punish your ignorance even though your ignorance of the law is inevitable given the sheer volume of what you're expected to know.

This situation is inherently unjust. Ignorance is no excuse, but at the same time ignorance is inevitable? This is a far cry from God's design.

Even lawyers have to specialise because it simply isn't possible for any one human to actually know all the laws. If those who make a *career* out of the law are still ignorant, what hope do the rest of us have?

Given that God is a God of justice, to say our current system is 'inherently unjust' is the same as saying it is inherently ungodly.

God never meant for it to be that way, He gave us laws that could be read in a few days and a system of arbitration for disputes...

And nothing more.

Of course, some people protest that our world is more complicated now, but the principles of justice remain the same! If you 'need' 40,000 laws then what you actually need is people who can write better and simpler laws, and fewer of them.

This is a universally understood truth and in the 1st Century BC Marcus Tillius Cicero said:

"The more laws, the less justice."

And we know that God agrees because when given His way, He designed a system with the fewest laws of any government in history.

The Old Testament records the ups and downs of this system that God designed in the book of Judges. To say it was a mixed bag is an understatement, but then again the same is true of our system today!

Godly judges brought justice and prosperity; evil and corrupt judges brought God's judgement *against* Israel, and poverty or even captivity usually followed soon after.

Even in God's design for government things were often awful and the government was often corrupt because all of us, including those of us who work in our government, are subject to the effects of the fall and of sin in the world.

Some may seize on the failures of the system in Judges as 'proof' that it doesn't work, that God got it wrong, but the truth is that: *No government can ever be better than the people in it.*

It's even worse in modern times because no *democratic* government can be better than the people who elect it.

This is the first uncomfortable truth we *must* accept as we consider how to obey God in a fallen world: the Fall, the first ever act of rebellion against God, which then allowed sin into our world and made Satan the 'Prince of the Power of the Air,' affects every person, every organisation, and *every* form of government, without exception.

Many people insist that because of the Fall people cannot be trusted with power over their own lives. That seems sensible, but if that's true then consider how much *more* it must be true that, because of the Fall, people cannot be trusted with power over the lives of *others.*

It was never God's intention to give people large amounts of power over each other; He knows we are utterly unfit to wield such power over our fellow man given how unfit we are to govern even ourselves!

God gave to the children of Israel a system of government that was the closest to a 'libertarian' government of any system we've seen before or since. God prescribed a government that was absolutely tiny and only had power to arbitrate disputes and enforce the relatively few laws that God had implemented.

It did *not* have the authority to do much else, and God made it this way on purpose.

By default every man and woman was free, provided they did no harm to another. That was God's design.

In comparison to the governments we have today, God's government was almost non-existent, yet God deemed it was sufficient for a nation of over one million people, and that no new laws would ever be needed! That was God's ideal, but even God's ideal went almost immediately wrong due to corruption and sinfulness in both the rulers and in the people under their rule, and the Israelites eventually decided that they knew better than God.

The period of Judges lasted about 350 years before in 1 Samuel 8 we read how the children of Israel decided that the ups and downs of their judges were proof there was a problem with the *system* that God had designed for their government—rather than a problem with the people *in* God's government, or even the people *being* governed.

It never crossed their mind that they may be getting the government they deserved... "No, no, that can't be right, *we* can't be the problem," they said, "God has made a mistake!" So they came to the prophet Samuel with a better idea.

There's a *lot* to unpack in the passage below, but I think it's important to start by simply reading 1 Samuel 8 for the full context, and then unpack it over the rest of this chapter.

And it came to pass, when Samuel was old, that he made his sons judges over Israel. Now the name of his first-born was Joel; and the name of his second, Abijah: they were judges in Beer-sheba. And his sons walked not in his ways, but turned aside after lucre (money)*, and took bribes, and perverted justice.*

Then all the elders of Israel gathered themselves together, and came to Samuel unto Ramah; and they said unto him, Behold, thou art old, and thy sons walk not in thy ways: now make us a king to judge us like all the nations.

But the thing displeased Samuel, when they said, Give us a king to judge us. And Samuel prayed unto Jehova. And Jehovah said unto Samuel, Listen to the voice of the people in all that they say unto you; for they have not rejected you, but they have rejected me, that I should not be king over them.

According to all the works which they have done since the day that I brought them up out of Egypt even unto this day, in that they have forsaken me, and served other gods, so do they also unto you.

Now listen to their voice: but you will protest solemnly unto them, and will show them the manner of the king that shall reign over them.

And Samuel told all the words of Jehovah unto the people that asked of him a king. And he said, This will be the manner of the king that shall reign over you: he will take your sons, and appoint them unto him, for his chariots, and to be his horsemen; and they shall run before his chariots; and he will appoint them unto him for captains of thousands, and captains of fifties; and he will set some to plow his ground, and to reap his harvest, and to make his instruments of war, and the instruments of his chariots· And he will take your daughters to be perfumers, and to be cooks, and to be bakers. And he will take your fields, and your vineyards, and your oliveyards, even the best of them, and give them to his servants. And he will take the tenth of your seed, and of your vineyards, and give to his officers, and to his servants. And he will take your men-servants, and your maid-servants, and your best young men, and your donkeys, and put them to his work. He will take the tenth of your flocks: and ye shall be his servants. And ye shall cry out in that day because of your king whom ye shall have chosen you; and Jehovah will not answer you in that day.

But the people refused to hearken unto the voice of Samuel; and they said, Nay: but we will have a king over us, that we also may be like all the nations, and that our king may judge us, and go out before us, and fight our battles. And Samuel heard all the words of the people, and he rehearsed them in the ears of Jehovah. And Jehovah said to Samuel, Hearken unto their voice, and make them a king.

— 1 Samuel 8:1-22

There's a *lot* to unpack, so let's work our way through it bit by bit.

Firstly, the children of Israel had a legitimate grievance: the two sons of Samuel *were* corrupt! This wasn't the first time this had happened in their history, but instead of repenting of their sin and asking God for better judges, the fed-up elders decided they could 'fix' God's design for government by copying the world around them.

Notice they said in verse 5, "Make us a king to judge us **like all the nations.**"

What was their reference point? Their grievance was genuine, but what was the source for their proposed solution? It was the nations around them—the pagan nations who did not worship God at all.

They didn't go to the prophet and say, "Ask God to find us judges who will serve God and do justice according to His word," nor did they say, "We repent of our sins and of being evil people and we'll turn back to God in the hope that He will restore justice in our land."

No, that would be too hard, that would require actual humility, that would require them to admit they were getting the government they deserved, that would require *them* to change. It was much easier to change the system.

Notice that God's immediate response was to compare their demand for a king to the *idol worship* of their ancestors! It's crystal clear in verses 7 and 8 that God sees their demand for a king as equal to the idol worship which their ancestors reverted to time and again in their journey out of Egypt and towards the Promised Land in which these Israelites now lived!

Remember those false gods which Joshua had challenged their ancestors to abandon and choose the living Lord God instead? Those man-made idols they had created with their own hands, instead of worshipping the God who gave them hands?

God immediately compares the Israelites' demand for a king with the worship of those exact same false gods.

Rejecting God's design for government is idolatry. Building a government of our own design is the same as building a Golden Calf.

I grew up thinking the commandment to "Have no other gods before me" was outdated—surely no one was practising idolatry in the 'modern' world?

After all, I'd never seen a golden calf, nor a shrine to Moloch, nor any idols built with human hands in the modern, sophisticated, enlightened West... had I?

I see it very differently now. I have become convinced that while idolatry *looks* very different today it's just as real, and just as serious, as it ever was.

Let's return to 1 Samuel 8.

From verse 11 on God is clearly warning them that this king they desire will *not* stop at just judging them. No, once you have a king he will do far more than judge, and God clearly warns that what the king will do is *bad.*

The rest of the passage is a warning from God that the king will take their sons and daughters into his service, paid for by taxes that are levied against them.

It's interesting that God likens a 10% tax to slavery in verse 17. Some versions say 'servants,' others say 'slaves,' but whatever the case God warns that it will get so bad that they will cry out to Him for relief from the very government they demanded and that God will not hear.

It's a stern warning, but it's brushed aside by the Israelites, who were sure they knew better. "No!" they said. "We will have a king over us so that we will be like the other nations, and the king will judge us and go out into battle before us."

How foolish. Their yard-stick for comparison was not God's design and God's best, but rather was whatever they saw other nations doing—man's best.

They literally replaced God as their king with a mere man, and replaced God's wisdom for government with the best that man had to offer.

They created a man-made idol.

Notice that in verse 22 God gives them what they want. Sometimes that's what judgement looks like.

Notice the list of bad things that God *warns* the children of Israel they will suffer at the hands of a king: they will lose their sons to his armies and industry and their daughters to his palace and service. The king will make captains over them, whom the king will pay handsomely with stolen goods as he makes the people his slaves... err, I mean with "taxes which are the price of living in a civilised country"... sorry about that slip of the tongue...

Notice the King will uses taxes to pay these captains in order to ensure they will be more loyal to the king than they are to their own neighbours... the taxpayers.

What are those captains for? They're to enforce the new laws, rules, taxes, and servitude that the king will demand from 'his' people... laws, rules, taxes, and service that God never intended His people to suffer.

I'm going to labour this point because there's such a depth of truth in this passage if only we'll take it to heart. Scripture teaches clearly that it is God who gives us increase. The Bible says children are a blessing from God, it is God that gives us a harvest, and God who sets us free.

In contrast the king will take our children, take our harvest, and take our freedom.

To paraphrase the warning that God is giving in 2 Samuel 8, it's this:

"The government you are creating with your own hands will take from you the blessings that I (God) made for you with My hands."

Now, that is not Scripture, it's my paraphrase, and you're welcome to disagree with it, but my reading of that passage is that God says, "Hey, you can have it, but be careful what you wish for."

Rejecting God's design for government is no mere administrative change; it's a rejection of the created order and will, by its nature, cause you to miss out on God's best for you… or worse.

Government-God Complex

In our post-enlightenment, post-Christian world where 'God is dead,' the Ten Commandments have been largely hidden from view, politicians no longer feel the need to flash their 'Christian' credentials, and secularism is the order of the day, the dirty little secret is that governments still believe in God... they believe it's them!

Allow me to illustrate.

Governments today believe that they can *change* what is right and what is wrong by changing the law.

The idea that right and wrong changes when the law changes is vastly different to the idea that right and wrong are constant and it is a law-maker's job to ensure the law reflects what is *already* right and wrong.

The idea that governments can *change* right and wrong is madness, utterly absurd to anyone who accepts the existence of a Creator God and therefore the concept of absolute right and wrong, yet the idea that a government can 'change' right and wrong is accepted by almost everyone today—certainly everyone in our political and justice system.

It's a philosophy known as 'legal positivism' and I discussed it in detail in my first book, *Good People Break Bad Laws*. I won't spend time talking about it here except to say that it's a 'might makes right' view of the law. The fact that a government *can* pass and enforce a law is taken as proof that it is 'right.' This is an idolatrous concept of 'right and wrong' which rejects the idea of a 'higher law,' or law of God, and simply holds that if the government can write and enforce a law then that is what's right. If the government changes the law, they automatically change what is right and what is wrong.

Our governments also believe that nothing is outside their jurisdiction. Nothing is outside their reach; nothing is truly 'private property' anymore—not your income, not your relationships, not your words, not your beliefs, not even your prayers anymore. *Nothing* is beyond the reach of a government if they, in their exclusive and infinite wisdom, decide they should be involved.

Have you noticed that you can barely breathe these days without needing some piece of paper giving you permission? To work you need a Tax File Number (Social Security number in the US), while the business employing you has to file a tonne of paperwork plus have council permission to operate in a correctly zoned premises with up-to-date inspections and certifications and insurances, and the list goes on. In Australia there are over 24,000 different occupational licenses... Did you know there were 24,000 different occupations?

There are few jobs left that you'd be legally able to do without first getting a government permit, an accreditation, or permission from one or more levels of government or some government-created bureaucracy. There's a license to fish, a permit to camp, and permission from 'traditional owners' to bushwalk or rock-climb, while you're being watched and warned and threatened and punished every moment of every day on the roads, the footpaths, the parks and even the beaches.

You can't build a house or significantly modify your own property without begging for permission first, a process which can easily take six months in Australia! And every single item you use within that extension or renovation has to have some sort of approval or 'standards' accreditation.

Then, of course, you're charged tens of thousands of dollars in 'stamp duty' for updating the titles office on the change of property ownership, taxes on the loan, excise on the insurance, and rates to council to pay for services whether you use them or not, and in many jurisdictions you also then 'owe' the government a percentage of the property value as a 'land tax.' And if you can't pay that tax? Well you'd better sell up and leave your property. The government's claim to 'its share' of your property value takes precedence over your claim to keep it. If you can't pay them for the 'privilege' of owning it, you can't keep it.

The concept of 'private property' doesn't exist anymore. You pay for your 'property' but you never own it.

God never intended it to be that way, and we know from Scripture that He would be horrified by the way that widows and retirees and the working poor are being kept poor and even forced out of their homes by the fees, charges, and taxes, levied against their 'private property.'

Your medical options are completely controlled by the government—everything from the doctors and nurses you see to the premises they use and the medicines they offer has to be approved and accredited by the government. Any doctor that deviates from the government-approved protocols risks deregistration, prison, or worse.

Your education was almost completely dictated by the government, including the class sizes, curriculum, premises, teachers' accreditations, testing, options for further education, and more.

And to pay for it all you have to pay income tax, GST (or VAT), land tax (on the land you 'own'), various stamp duties, and fees and charges and hidden taxes, all under threat of violence if you don't comply, and with absolutely no financial privacy whatsoever. The government can simply come in and demand whatever information they like and punish you if they *think* you're lying. In Australia, if they accuse you of lying on your taxes *they* don't have to prove it, *you* have to prove them wrong!

Some people defend this absurdity by arguing that the government is just keeping us safe—it's ensuring that things are of a decent standard and keeping 'bad apples' from taking advantage.

That's not the government's job, and allowing the government to have that kind of power is not just dangerous, it's idolatry. And it begs the question... what happens when the government *becomes* the bad apple?

Today the government is not content to simply control and micromanage every aspect of our physical and financial lives... now they exercise complete control over our words, thoughts, prayers, and beliefs as well.

For decades we've seen a trend around the world of a new genre of 'blasphemy' laws, cleverly disguised as anti-discrimination laws.

Back in the 'bad old days' when humans were superstitious and religious, 'blasphemy laws' were used to punish people who didn't agree with the dominant beliefs of the day. 'Heretics' were punished through public humiliation, excommunication, prosecution, and even execution.

But we don't do that any more... right?

Try stating that marriage is only between a man and a woman, that people's gender is defined by their chromosomes, or that 'traditional owners' and 'first nations' people have no special connection to 'country.'

You'll soon find yourself subjected to public humiliation, excommunication (from your job, your clients, your social circles, your social media accounts, your friends and family groups), prosecution (thanks to anti-discrimination laws), and execut... OK, so we haven't quite got to executions yet, but give it time!

You're a Heretic for saying any one of these things.

You may think I'm over-stating the case. I wish I were.

In my former home state of Victoria, Australia, there are laws against praying for someone to accept their gender as defined by their chromosomes—their gender as they were created by God.

The legislation is called the 'Change Suppression Practices Legislative Ban' and it means that if someone comes to you and expresses confusion or uncertainty about their gender and you say or *pray* anything that doesn't directly affirm their desire to 'transition' then you're a criminal.

Simply urging them to wait a while, to pray about it, to perhaps read the parts of the Bible about how God knew us before we were born and formed us in the womb and how He made us exactly how He intended us to be... just doing any of those things would make you a *criminal.*

It's important to emphasise: *criminal.*

This is not like the anti-discrimination laws we've had for some time in Australia which make it a *civil* offence to offend or 'vilify' people on the basis of protected traits like their race or their sexuality or their gender identity. In those cases someone has to *want* to sue you, and the penalties are strictly civil (*i.e.* money).

In the case of the 'Change Suppression Practices Legislative Ban' it's a *criminal* offence, and that distinction matters because it means the government can prosecute you even if the person you spoke to and prayed for was *happy* about it—even if they don't *want* you to be prosecuted—*and* it opens up the possibility of criminal punishments including prison and a criminal record, for *praying.*

Maybe such laws haven't yet arrived where you are, but I promise you it's only a matter of time, because the same idolatrous spirit is at work behind all governments and it's going to take a move of God to change the current trend. More on that later.

Today the government simply does what it likes and insists it's right (legal positivism), and more than that, the government insists if you don't support it then you're not just incorrect, you're evil. Because the government is God.

Here in Australia we have a new state-sponsored religion in the form of an indigenous Aboriginal paganism based on a

'Dreamtime' creation theology. If you doubt that it's a state-sponsored religion, try hiring a government facility without being forced to participate in some form of 'acknowledgement of country' ceremony which acknowledges indigenous elders 'past, present, and emerging,' a reference to indigenous beliefs that their deceased elders are still with us.

If you're a company wanting to supply things to the Australian Government you'd better have an 'acknowledgement' of the 'first peoples' on your website and probably some sort of affirmative action policy showing that you preferentially hire indigenous Australians regardless of the presence of more qualified candidates elsewhere, and if you work for the government don't you dare speak up about the fact that you're being forced to practice a religion against your will... at least, not if you'd like to keep your job.

Now taxpayers dollars are being spent to build an altar... err sorry, 'smoking ceremony dish,' at a new Victorian train station. A State funded altar for a State sanctioned religion.

The same is true of transgenderism. Speaking against it is blasphemy, pure and simple, and the government will force you to believe, or at least appear to believe, whatever they insist is true and right this week... which is different to what was true and right last week, and will change again at any moment in the future.

But even still we haven't covered the full horror of the government-god complex.

As the 'good conservative' that I was raised to be, I was taught that you must agree to fight the government's wars, or at least fund them. It was 'right' to prioritise the protection of your government above your own life if you're ordered to do so. And how dare you question whether your government is actually worthy of such a sacrifice, you heretic! How dare you question the justice or necessity of any war your government has become entangled in!

The government knows better than you!

And you will surrender to the government as much of your income as they deem right and be grateful for what they benevolently leave in your bank account; you will support and fund every social program, *especially* those that involve killing unborn children or mutilating the genitals of children; you will submit to their 'justice' system, no matter how unjust; you will support without question every use of violence by anyone with a badge or a uniform; and of course, you will condemn without hesitation anyone who questions the rightness of your idol.

Your government is your God, and don't you forget it.

There is nothing, *nothing*, outside of their jurisdiction, and questioning their authority to do anything and everything they like is the worst crime of all.

And this remains true regardless of which political party is in power.

It amuses me greatly, in a dark sort of a way, when I hear people wailing about how the 'other' side of politics are 'literally Hitler' in one breath, and then attempting to expand the power of government in the next.

Don't they realise that it's only a matter of time before the 'other side' wields all of that power?

If it's true that electing the 'wrong' person would destroy our country due to their unchecked abuse of government power, perhaps it's time to wake up to the fact that the government has *too much power*.

Can you see the absurdity of thinking that fallen man cannot be trusted with freedom, and so instead entrusting fallen men (and women) with *power* instead?

And no, it really doesn't make much difference which 'side' is in power. Both 'sides' agree that the government has the power to do whatever the government, in its infinite wisdom, deems right, necessary, or best.

The 'progressive' side of politics use the government to make everyone live according to their ideal, while the 'conservative' side of politics use the government to make everyone... live according to their ideal!

Yes, their respective 'ideal' is very different, but underneath the differing appearances is absolute agreement on *both* sides that the government has the authority to *make* people live the 'right' way... whatever the 'right' way is this week.

God never intended for it to be this way and God warned the Israelites, and through them He warned us, of the terrible consequences of making the government god.

The Names of God

God takes His name so seriously that one of the Ten Commandments is to not take His name in vain.

But God's name is far more than just something we shouldn't blaspheme. For example, when David, the man after God's own heart, prayed for God's favour, deliverance, and blessing, he often asked God to answer his prayers "for Your name's sake" [Psalm 23; Psalm 143].

God gives Himself many names because He is a God with many facets, and He uses His various names to help us to understand our relationship with Him and the various ways in which we can relate to and depend on Him.

In the Old Testament we see God refer to Himself in literally dozens of different ways from 'Jehovah' to 'Elohim' to 'El-Shaddai.' There are entire studies you can do on the names of God, but I'm going to focus specifically on the seven most used 'Jehovah'-based names.

God makes promises to us in His own name, promises to be there for us and to meet our needs in very specific ways... ways which our governments have explicitly sought to undermine and usurp as they have tried to replace God in our lives.

The government commits blasphemy by trying to usurp each of the names of God and claim them for itself.

Jehovah Jireh — The Lord Will Provide

God makes it very clear that we are supposed to look to Him for our provision in life. This isn't some 'blab it and grab it' prosperity doctrine, it's a recognition that God as the creator of the universe is the giver of all life and the giver of all good gifts.

So if, as I claim, governments are seeking to replace God, it stands to reason that we would see governments promising to be our providers in place of God... and that is *exactly* what we see.

The obvious example is governments promising to provide welfare when we're in need. What God intended to be accomplished through interpersonal charity and trust in Him, government now 'does for us' through welfare, creating trust in government.

A less obvious example is when governments claim to 'create jobs' and 'manage the economy,' always taking credit for the good times and finding external factors to blame for the bad, while encouraging you to accept its 'help' in the form of corporate handouts, middle class welfare, and the poverty-industrial-complex of unemployment benefits, in the bad times.

This means that whether you're welfare dependent or self-sufficient the government still insists that it is your provider. They are your Government-Jireh.

Progressive politicians view your income, capital gains, retirement savings, investment returns, and all other income as belonging to the government first. You can keep whatever the government decides to leave for you.

They believe you 'owe' whatever taxes, fees, and charges they levy because the government 'provided' for you the conditions within which you made that money. And really, they're being nice by letting you keep any of it at all!

US Democrat Elizabeth Warren summed up this mentality perfectly: *"There is nobody in this country who got rich on his own—nobody. You built a factory out there? Good for you. But I want to be clear. You moved your goods to market on the roads the rest of us paid for. You hired workers the rest of us paid to educate. You were safe in your factory because of police-forces and fire-forces that the rest of us paid for. You didn't have to worry that marauding bands would come and seize everything at your factory—and hire someone to protect against this—because of the work the rest of us did. Now look, you built a factory and it turned into something terrific, or a great idea. God bless—keep a big hunk of it. But part of the underlying social contract is, you take a hunk of that and pay forward for the next kid who comes along."*

Surely only a greedy, uncaring, and heartless person could object to such reasoning, right?

Soon-to-be-President Barack Obama echoed that sentiment in his now infamous 'You didn't build that' speech. He was misquoted as having said that business owners didn't build their businesses. That's *not* what he said; what he said was that business owners didn't build the infrastructure around their businesses, which they then used and depended on to operate their business. Obama pointed out that that surrounding infrastructure was built by others.

There are two great deceptions at the heart of that logic, which are the same two deceptions that lie at the heart of government's idolatrous claim to be our provider.

Displacement:

The first deception is *displacement.* The government provides only that which it actively *stops* others from providing first!

The reason 'the government' provides things like roads and police and education for your employees is because they stopped others from doing so long ago.

History clearly shows that roads, railways, charities, universities, hospitals for the poor... all of that existed before government got involved.

So why do we 'need' the government to do all these things today? How come there aren't enough private charities, charitable hospitals, privately funded roads and railways, and the like, today? Because the government has usurped its own people and displaced us from performing those functions without them.

A Twitter (X) user Geoff Graham summed this up beautifully in a viral tweet which said, *"If children started school at six months old and their teachers gave them walking lessons, within a single generation people would come to believe that humans couldn't learn to walk without going to school."*

The deception is the belief that if the government didn't do it then *it wouldn't be done.* That *only* the government can do it.

This same deception lies at the heart of government interventions of every kind today. There's so much we think we *cannot do* without their help—roads, charity, education—but history tells us we *did* do all those things before the government got involved!

People are quick to point out, "You wouldn't want to have lived in a poor house or had surgery in 'charity' hospitals in the 1800s!"

And that's true, I wouldn't! But what these people miss is that I wouldn't have wanted to live in a palace in the 1800s either! Before penicillin, telephones, headache tablets, aeroplanes, or flushing toilets? No, thanks!

A 2016 article in *The Atlantic*, "America in 1915: Long Hours, Crowded Houses, Death by Trolley" by Derek Thompson, drives this point home. In 1915 the age of steam was well advanced but almost every other technology, including electricity, medical, communication, and vehicular transport, was in its infancy. No amount of money would entice most modern Westerners, even those we consider 'poor' in the West, to swap with the richest man on earth in the early 20th Century, and go without phones, antibiotics, cars, air conditioners, movies, the internet, or chocolate.

This means that when we compare modern government welfare, education, housing, and healthcare with pre-government intervention times, we must account for the vast difference in overall living standards and technology.

Compared to the living standards of their time, the charities which operated *privately*, before the government took over and convinced us that *only* they could provide a safety net, were adequate. The charity hospitals were decent hospitals *by the standards of their time*. And by the late 1800s the privately funded railways were marvels of technology which were transforming the lives of the rich and poor, largely without any government involvement.

Early industrialists and railway pioneers were the Elon Musks of their time. Love him or hate him, Musk is completely transforming our world *from the private sector.* That's how it was *always* done until the government came along and told us that it couldn't be.

So the government is simply claiming credit for doing the things it actively *stopped or displaced others* from doing in the first place.

To quote Harry Browne, *"The government is good at one thing. It knows how to break your legs, and then hand you a crutch and say, 'See, if it weren't for the government, you wouldn't be able to walk.'"*

I'd say it this way: *"The government is good at one thing. It knows how to take from you the bounty God has provided, eat most of it, hand you the crumbs and say, 'See? If it weren't for the government you'd starve.'"*

For anyone who doubts that the private sector could and would provide everything we need, including roads, parks, healthcare, and security, consider the example of a large shopping mall. It's completely privately owned, yet on that land you'll find roads, multi-story car parking, parks and play areas for kids, food courts that are cleaned continuously, toilets and baby change rooms, and ample security services. Most of it is free (parking, playgrounds, toilets, air conditioning, security, etc) and *none* of it is being provided by government! It's all been provided by a private owner who wants to make a profit!

Yep, *money* is why shopping centres provide you with roads, parking, play areas, toilets, sanitation, security, and all the other things that governments claim that *only* they can provide.

Money.

And that's how God intended it to be.

1 Timothy 6:10 says, *"The love of money is a root of all kinds of evil,"* and people often misquote it as, *"Money is the root of all evil."* But it's not the money itself, it's the *love* of money that is the issue.

Making money via profit from trading with others and providing value to your fellow human beings is *good*, and the Bible says so, as we'll see in a moment.

This 'profit motive' (which is what the private sector is based on) is the best possible incentive for people to help and provide for each other's needs. Taking away that incentive, that 'profit motive,' by bullying out the private sector and making something a 'public good' twists God's design into Satan's deception with devastating consequences.

I know that sounds like heresy, so let me explain.

The government claims to be your provider and that 'only' the government could provide you with roads, parking, security, parks, healthcare, and the like, but like all deceptions and deviations from God's created order, like all of Satan's counterfeits to God's design, the government actually steals, kills, and destroys that which was provided by God's design.

God's design for how He would meet your needs is clearly explained in Scripture: it's private trade *for profit*.

God primarily *provides* through our work and mutually beneficial trade with our fellow human beings.

I do not dismiss the miraculous at all, but in the main it is clear in Scripture that God's design for how you eat, put a roof over your head, provide for your children, your health, and your old age is through the creation of value followed by mutually beneficial trade with others.

When government steps in it is displacing these voluntary trades and stopping us from providing for ourselves and for each other's needs.

'Displacement' is the first reason the government is lying when it claims credit for 'providing' for you—*i.e.*, claiming only it can do things that can actually be done better privately and 'for profit.'

Opportunity Cost:

The second deception is one of 'opportunity cost.' The bold version of this lie is that government services are 'free,' the more subtle version of this lie is that when government taxes and spends that it 'creates value,' 'creates jobs,' or 'stimulates the economy.'

That's a lie. Satan comes to steal, kill, and destroy, and governments taxing and spending is one of Satan's most powerful tools for all of the above.

The reason it's a lie is that government funds its actions by taking money away from people who *actually* meet the needs of others (through God's design of work and mutually beneficial trade) and 'gives it back' in the form of goods and services which are not necessarily wanted, beneficial, or good value.

In short, the government 'provides' things that people may or may not want by taking money from people who would have spent or invested it in things of actual value.

Government is 'providing' by coercion and threat what God intended to be provided through voluntary trade and mutual profit.

You'll see this truth throughout Scripture, but the most in-your-face example is Proverbs 31.

People often object to Proverbs 31 because they think it's all about telling women to be a demure 1950s-style housewife, but nothing could be further from the truth!

Consider just how empowered, independent, and strong this woman is, and look at just how involved in buying and selling land and merchandise and *making profit* she is:

She seeks wool and flax and works with willing hands. She is like the ships of the merchant, she brings her food from far away. She rises while it is still night and provides food for her household and ***tasks for her servant-girls****. She* ***considers a field and buys it****; with the fruit of her hands* ***she plants a vineyard****. She girds herself with strength and makes her arms strong. She perceives that* ***her merchandise is profitable****. Her lamp does not go out at night. She puts her hands to the distaff, and her hands hold the spindle.* ***She opens her hand to the poor, and reaches out her hands to the needy****. She is not afraid for her household when it snows, for* ***all her household are clothed in crimson****...*

... she makes linen garments ***and sells them; she supplies the merchant with sashes****.*

— Proverbs 31:13-21, 24

This is an empowered and successful businesswoman if ever I saw one! Notice how much of the praise directed to her is based on the way she creates value and trades with others, in accordance with God's design for how He is our provider, our Jehovah Jireh.

The details of free markets are beyond the scope of this book. However, there are a few principles which can be seen with any clear-eyed reading of Scripture as a whole and of Proverbs 31 in particular:

1. God approves of private property—He outlaws theft and breaking and entering and demands recompense for damage to property, all affirming that God allows and protects private property.
2. In Proverbs 31 God explicitly condones the ownership of property, buying and selling of land, operating of private businesses, manufacturing and trading of goods, and employing of staff.
3. God approves of voluntary free trade, or 'buying, selling, and making gain,' provided it is done with honesty, or 'just weights' [Proverbs 20:23].

Private property and free markets are not some 'Capitalist' idea that was invented in the last few hundred years. Capitalism is simply private property and voluntary trade and it was invented by God and has been practised since the first time a fish was swapped for some firewood.

'Capitalism' is re-invented every day in the schoolyard as children swap lunches according to their likes and dislikes, and free trade is baked in to God's design as our provider, our Jehovah Jireh.

God declares that He is our provider, but even so He is also incredibly clear that each of us has a responsibility to work hard to provide for ourselves and those we serve, such as our families and children.

Whilst God advocates for giving to the poor, He never approves of laziness or welfare dependence. In fact, one of the harshest condemnations in the New Testament is for those who do not provide for their families:

But those who won't care for their relatives, especially those in their own household, have denied the true faith. Such people are worse than unbelievers.

— 1 Timothy 5:8

The original Greek word translated 'care' in the verse is *pronoeó*, or literally, 'to foresee.' In other words, this is an instruction to foresee and provide for your family's needs in a timely fashion, or be *worse* than an unbeliever.

Our God, Jehovah Jireh, our *provider*, commands us to get to work and create products or services that others will want to trade with us for. That's not a contradiction to God as our provider, that is His design—His *way* of providing.

The Idol of Welfare.

When I speak on Capitalism and God's instructions to provide for ourselves and our loved ones, someone will invariably object that we 'need' welfare, and that I'm uncaring and heartless for advocating God's design.

But God *is* love, He cares deeply for every single human being, especially the poor and needy, yet never in Scripture, Old Testament or New, do we see God instructing or advocating for centralised government-run welfare. Never.

Private charity? Yes. Government *Welfare*? No.

Leviticus gives an example of how God intended for the poor and needy to be provided for via private means:

When you reap the harvest of your land, you shall not wholly reap the corners of your field when you reap, nor shall you gather any gleaning from your harvest. You shall leave them for the poor and for the stranger: I am the LORD your God.

— Leviticus 23:22

The needs of the poor, of immigrants and of travellers, was supposed to be met out of the abundance of *private* enterprise. That was God's design, but we thought we knew better.

Remember that too much government is a perversion of God's created order. It's idolatry. Making the government do what God told *us* to do is a rejection of God as our king and the creation of an idol in His place.

Government-Jireh is Satan's counterfeit and the end result will always be that he steals, kills, and destroys.

The lie is that we can *better* care for the poor through government welfare than through God's design of work and voluntary trade (which includes voluntary charity). But the reality is that government is perpetuating poverty and creating a trap that is destroying future generations.

This is a theme we will see as we go on in this book: Government takes God's place, perverts His ways, and steals, kills, and destroys.

Charity is something we are all called to practice—we must not abandon the poor, the widows, the orphans, or the oppressed, and we must not stop our ear "at the cry of the poor" or else we will also "cry out in poverty and not be heard" [Proverbs 21:13].

We are called to practice charity as individuals, as families, and as communities of believers, such as in the context of the Church, but never in Scripture are we instructed to practice welfare through the mechanism of government.

This is no petty distinction or administrative change. The shift from charity to welfare is a shift from a *relationship of value* between the giver and the receiver to a soulless and uncaring system that actually perpetuates poverty.

It's a shift from *responsibility* to *entitlement.*

It is as profound as the difference between relationship with God and religiosity. They can look the same from the outside, but in reality they are opposites.

Charity is a hand *up* that brings relationship between the giver and receiver and responsibility to the recipient to do all they can to emerge from their poverty and begin to create value in accordance with God's design. Welfare is a hand *out* that encourages lifelong dependency on valueless consumption and *creates poverty for all.*

Welfare *creates poverty* because it allows recipients to consume value created by others with no obligation on them to create value in return!

Welfare is a perversion of God's design for charity *and* as we would expect it actually *steals* value from our community and *destroys* those who are receiving the welfare!

Charity counts itself successful when it lifts people up so they no longer need charity. Welfare counts itself successful if more people than ever are depending on it.

Let me cut to the chase: *Choosing* to consume value without even *trying* to create value in return is defiance of God's created order, and anyone who *enables* such valueless consumption is defying God no matter how good their intentions are.

I'll immediately note that the Bible allows for people to make mistakes or have setbacks, fall on hard times, and *need* charity. It also allows for people with disabilities or other difficulties to depend on charity as well, but it *does not* allow for people who *could* produce value to *choose* not to.

It's the choice that is the key distinction here. Anyone can fall on hard times, become sick, injured, or disabled, or genuinely *need* charity for valid reasons. But even in such circumstances it is God's design for us to work and trade as much as we *can*, within the realities of our circumstances.

We *all* have a responsibility before God to produce as much value as we can within our circumstances and abilities, and only the most unfortunate or disabled should ever be allowed to live permanently off the good graces of charity. Everyone else *must* be expected to do what work they *can* to produce whatever value is possible for them, with charity making up the shortfall for their survival.

This is a hard word in Western democracies because the Welfare State has become an idol, and demanding that welfare recipients do what they *can* do is blasphemy.

But if enabling valueless consumption is a defiance of God's created order then welfare is actually idolatry.

God's purpose for charity is to meet *only* the most essential needs for the survival of people who would otherwise go without food, water, shelter, clothing, or basic emergency medical care. If people want more than mere survival, if they want to be comfortable, to have a car, new shoes every six months, or a bigger tv, then they must work for it.

God says so.

First, remember that God, Jehovah Jireh, is our provider [Genesis 22, Philippians 4:19, etc.].

Second, as our provider, God instructed us to work and create things of value that we can trade with each other [Proverbs 31], and that if we don't then we're worse than an unbeliever [1 Timothy 5:8]. We are supposed to work and trade to create a surplus of value to bless future generations with after we die [Proverbs 13:22].

It is simultaneously true that God is our provider, our Jehovah Jireh, *and* that His provision will mostly come through work and trade amongst ourselves. That is how He designed it.

I say this without discounting that from time to time God does intervene in supernatural ways, but these are the exception rather than the rule. Even then, usually when supernatural provision comes it is often in the form of a gift from another person who *is able to give because of their own abundance of work and trade* in accordance with God's created order. *I.e.*, even the supernatural answer to prayer usually (but not always) comes out of the abundance from someone else obeying God's instructions to work and trade.

Look around you. The wealth that we take for granted in the modern Western world is the result of the work and trade which was carried out by past generations on our behalf. It is an inheritance left to us by our forebears who, whether they knew it or not, were obeying God's designed order for how He would provide for us and were leaving an inheritance to their children's children—us!

The infrastructure, technologies, and ideas which we benefit from every day are a legacy left to us by our forebears who *created more value than they consumed.*

We know that's true because we see all around us the fruits of *their* labours, the infrastructure, the technology, the art, and the ideas... all the value left behind by men and women who are now dead but created more value than they consumed in their lifetimes.

The equation is simple. If, on average, people *create* more value (through their work and trade) than they consume, then the world becomes a wealthier place and we leave an inheritance to our children's children.

However if, on average, people *consume* more value than they create then the world becomes a poorer place and future generations suffer.

Proverbs 13:22 says, *"A good man leaves an inheritance to his children's children."*

How? By working and trading to create more value than he consumes. The wealth we enjoy today is because we stand on the shoulders of generations of 'good men' (and women) who left us with an amazing inheritance. And the inheritance isn't just in the form of a 'will' with a payout to actual descendants, it's also in the form of the legacy of infrastructure, art, ideas, and more.

That is God's design for the economy, for wealth, for the building and prosperity of cultures and civilisations, *and* for charity.

I take it to be self-evident that it means that we should act to intervene on behalf of anyone who is at risk of starvation, of death due to bad water (sadly still a problem in some parts of the world today), or of death due to exposure either from lack of clothing or lack of shelter, and based on the parable of the Good Samaritan [Luke 10:25-37] I take it that we have a responsibility to intervene with appropriate emergency medical care where the need arises.

Again, the Bible doesn't say that the *government* has a responsibility to intervene, it says that *we* do.

OK, so God requires us to leave an inheritance to our children's children, which comes out of the wealth we create by working and trading, *and* God requires us to be able to help the poor and needy with *charity* as the need arises as well, and this charity is supposed to come out of the abundance that comes out of our work and trade.

This is the design that God, as our provider, gave to us. So far, so good.

There's one more piece of the puzzle we need to discuss before we arrive at some very uncomfortable conclusions.

If my thesis is correct and our government is an idol which is usurping and twisting God's created order, then it follows that the outcomes from government welfare will be perverse. We know that Satan comes to steal, kill, and destroy. So if welfare really is an idol, a Satanic perversion of God's created order, then it must result in some combination of stealing, killing, or destroying.

And that's exactly what we see.

Welfare is directly responsible for enormous destruction of wealth and is impoverishing future generations, stealing away the inheritance we were supposed to leave for them.

Before you stone me as a heretic let's put that last puzzle piece in place: Value.

Every transaction has two sides. One side is the money that changes hands, the other side is the goods or services exchanged for that money, or the value.

Remember that trade is good because it's a part of God's created design for how He provides for us. In a truly free market, a market that works as God intended, all transactions are voluntary. If either party says 'no' then the transaction will not take place.

In a functioning free market every single transaction represents a moment in time when *both* sides of the transaction, the one spending the money and the one providing the goods or services, believe they are better off *after* the transaction than they were before.

Governments measure the money side of transactions *only*. They call it the 'GDP' or Gross Domestic Product. But the money is the *less* important side of any transaction. It's what is done in *exchange* for that money that matters.

The money changes hands and can be used again and again, it's not 'consumed' in a transaction, but on the other side of every transaction is the 'value,' or the thing being bought and sold. This is a product or service which someone is 'consuming.' It may be consumed all at once, like a meal, or it may last many decades, like a house, but the non-money side of the transaction is the *value* that is being exchanged for money, and it's the side of the transaction that matters.

In one time or place in history it might require one hundred dollarbucks (pick any currency you like) to buy dinner, in another it might require five dollarbucks. The number of dollarbucks exchanged is vastly different and yet exactly *one* belly was filled in return.

In Venezuela I paid over 500,000 Bolivars for lunch for ten people. I could have paid $500 for the same meal for ten in Australia, and in both transactions ten bellies would have been filled. The amount of 'dollarbucks' from one time or place to another isn't that important, it's the things being done in *return* for the money.

Consider what would happen if the government simply gave an order to add two extra 'zeros' onto the price of everything. The amount of money changing hands for a given good or service would jump up massively. A large McDonalds meal would cost $1,500 instead of $15 for the exact same product...

The amount of money changing hands goes up, but actual wealth, the way we live, is unchanged (or actually becomes worse because few people can afford anything).

So the money side of the economy is *less* important than the other side, the actual goods and services which make up our quality of life.

In other words, the bit that matters in every transaction and in the economy is the side of the transaction that the government *doesn't* measure.

If our instruction from God is to create more than we consume then it's not the dollars that are relevant, it's what we consume versus what we create.

The money *only* matters in as far as we got that money by creating equivalent *value* to replace the meal we're now using that money to buy. It's the value of the work we *did* for that money, and the value of the work that others are now doing in an effort to get that money *from* us, that actually makes the world a wealthier and better place.

Not the money, the value.

Money is useful because it is a *means of exchange* and because it is a *store of value,* which means that in a functioning economy it *represents value*.

I.e., if you have money to spend it (should be) because you have at some point in the past provided valuable goods or services to someone in exchange for that money.

In other words if you don't create value for others (in return for money) then you don't get to consume value created by others (because you have no money). But this *only* works in a world where money changing hands represents value that has been created, and therefore when someone *has* money it's proof they created value.

In such a world, if you don't provide value to others in return for their money then you soon have no money. You'll have to stop consuming because you have no money to give others in return for the value they have to offer.

You can't consume value if you don't first create some.

God's design of providing for our needs through work and trade stops people from over-consuming, or consuming more value than they create and stealing from future generations as a result.

Measuring the GDP, the *money* side of transactions leads us to miss the terrible consequences of government welfare because welfare payments are a transfer of money with *no value exchanged in return*.

Money is taken from taxpayers in return for no value, and is given to welfare recipients with *no obligation for them to create value in return.* Money moves from a taxpayer to the government to a welfare recipient, but no goods or services are provided, no value is created, and no legacy is left for our children's children.

The recipient of the payment, who created no value in return for it, is now free to spend that money in the consumption of value created by others. The fact that they have money is *supposed* to function as proof that they have created value, to stop them from consuming more than they create at the expense of future generations, but thanks to the government they haven't had to do that.

Now, at this point I know that you may very well be objecting, "What about people with disabilities?" or more generally, "What about people who have a valid reason why they can't create economic value like the rest of us?" and you're absolutely right to ask the question.

I'll say it again, no one should go hungry, drink bad water, or suffer from a lack of clothing or shelter or basic medical care in an emergency.

Scripture clearly teaches us to look after the poor, widows, orphans, disabled, injured... basically any category of person who, under their current circumstances, cannot reasonably be expected to provide for themselves economically.

Or to say it another way, God calls on us to share the value *we* have created through our work and trade with those who cannot reasonably be expected to create value equal to or greater than what they need to consume in order to have the essentials for life.

I am not advocating for leaving people to suffer in the gutter or to die from a lack of the most basic essentials for life.

Charity is when people give out of the abundance of the value *they* created, and when charity is done right it builds relationship and accountability for the recipient, leading people to lift themselves up out of poverty, or at the very least to do what they *can* do within the limitations of their physical or mental or situational capacity.

It's very rare that someone truly can do *nothing* to create value. It does happen, and those people should be fully cared for regardless, but in the vast majority of cases people can do *something,* to create *some* value, and people should always be expected to do what they can.

In contrast, welfare incentivises people to take all that they can take, in return for nothing.

Charity, done right, helps people get out of poverty, while welfare traps people in it *and* destroys the wealth of future generations.

It's beyond the scope of this book to address the welfare trap, the way that the state perpetuates welfare dependency, or the economic devastation we are now facing due to government debt and money printing, but I think you can probably look out your window and see that for yourself.

I will say this, though: while God says that a righteous man, that is, one who follows God's design for work and trade, leaves an inheritance to his children's children, what *we're* leaving to our children is debt.

I was born in the 1980s and my generation were given good infrastructure with little to no debt in Australia, but we are leaving crumbling infrastructure with tens of thousands of dollars of debt hanging over the head of every newborn child from the moment they are born.

The numbers are staggering. According to the United Nations Conference on Trade and Development, global public debt passed $100 Trillion in 2024.

Let's try and wrap our minds around that insane number by converting dollars to seconds.

100,000,000,000,000 seconds is over 3 MILLION years.

Nope, I still can't grasp it. Let's try to break it down per-person and see if that helps.

According to the usdebtclock.org website the debt per person in the USA is over $100,000USD and climbing fast. But not all US people are working and paying tax, so actually that debt has to be repaid by the less than 40% of the population that pays tax and therefore the debt per taxpayer is actually over $270,000USD.

But that's just the start, because governments don't only have debt, they also make *promises they can't keep.* These promises are almost exclusively welfare, healthcare, and retirement related, and whilst this isn't debt today, it is money they're going to need in the foreseeable future.

The *unfunded liabilities* per-person in the US is an astronomical $650,000USD+, which means the unfunded liabilities per *taxpayer* amount to more than $1,600,000 for each and every taxpayer.

Every child born in the US is born with that hanging over their head.

Forget leaving an inheritance to our children's children; we're living large on *their* credit card, and giving them very little to show for it.

Satan has perverted God's ways, set up an idol of Government-Jireh, and has stolen, killed, and destroyed our children's future via our idolatry.

God said He was our Jehovah Jireh, our provider. But the government promised to replace Him and be our provider instead, to meet our needs, to ensure our prosperity, to create a safety net we could depend on in times of crisis in our lives… that was their promise.

In reality we have an economic system based on thin air (fiat currency) enabled by the threat of violence (try not paying taxes if you don't believe me) which perpetuates poverty (welfare trap), steals from future generations (intergenerational debt), and is primed for yet another downturn.

Is this what God wanted for us? Is this what God promised when He said He would be our provider?

Of course not. This is the consequences of our idolatry.

This is what happens when we take the name of the Lord our God in vain.

Government as Jehovah

Let's look at a few more of God's names:

Jehovah Nissi — The Lord is your refuge
Jehovah Shalom — The Lord is your peace
Jehovah Ra'ah — The Lord is your way and shepherd
Jehovah Tsidkenu — The Lord is your righteousness
Jehovah Shammah — The Lord is ever-there (or ever present)
Jehovah Rapha — The Lord is your healer — a name with particular relevance to our moment in history.

For each of these 'Jehovah'-based names the government has now directly encroached onto God's appointed title and claimed that role for itself.

Every. Single. One.

Government-Nissi:
Who now considers itself your refuge and defender? The government, of course.

Government-Shalom:
Peace comes not from God but from compliance with government. Only total compliance with the government's diktats can bring you peace from their ever-present enforcers.

Government-Ra'ah:
You are shepherded in the right 'way' by attending government schools and completing their vocational training, as well as accepting whatever the latest approved views are on social issues such as gender.

Government-Tsidkenu:
You are deemed righteous or unrighteous by your government's

legal system, which long ago ceased to be about justice and is about enforcing compliance with the ever-changing rules. And by the way, those rules are *always* righteous, even though they're ever-changing—they were righteous before they changed *and* they're righteous afterwards, and don't you forget it!

Government-Shammah:
Our government is 'ever there.' Online and physical surveillance are normalised to the point that people get angry if you object.

We have allowed our government to become god in our society, not just metaphorically, but literally displacing and replacing every name that God gave Himself.

Everywhere you look, from our economic, legal, and education systems to our military, police, and everywhere else, the government has positioned itself at the tippy-top of the totem pole, in place of God.

Government can do all things, *must* do all things, nothing is beyond their reach, and nothing can be done *without* them.

To repeat the lovely quote from Geoff Graham: *"If children started school at six months old and their teachers gave them walking lessons, within a single generation people would come to believe that humans couldn't learn to walk without going to school."*

Within just a few generations we've become convinced that *only* government can do all the things which God said were His domain.

Today the government is worshipped as god in every area of life, but *nowhere* is this more true than Government-Rapha, the god of your healthcare.

Healthcare is a wonderful thing, and modern medicine is capable of performing what past generations would have regarded as miracles.

Surely we owe our longer life expectancy and amazing modern trauma care to the government, right? The government is the giver of healthcare, right? In countries like the UK with the NHS, Australia with Medicare, and the US with increasing efforts to introduce single-payer healthcare, *surely* it's a wonderful and good thing that the government has become our healer...?

Isn't it?

Many regard this as an open-and-shut case, and in the UK in particular the NHS is something of a cult, a sacred institution beyond reproach or question.

That's the perception, but as we'll see later in this book, perceptions often lag decades behind reality, and the reality is that government-run and government-funded healthcare has been perverted.

First we must make some distinctions and address an 'elephant in the room.'

It's important to acknowledge the tremendous improvement in life expectancy and overall health into old age that has taken place over the last 150 years. The data is crystal clear: we are living longer, and are healthier for longer, than at any other time since long before Christ.

It is often assumed that this must be because of modern medicine, and there is some truth to that, but the bulk of it is due to engineering.

Things like water treatment, sewage systems, and soap have saved far more lives than open heart surgery ever will.

The tremendous decline in diseases which used to ravage humanity is largely due to these engineering advancements, transport, and nutrition, *aided* by medicine.

If we set aside the last fifty years and the explosion of 'fake foods,' based on the fraudulent 'food pyramid' which we'll address in a moment, today you can eat a better diet of fresher and more nutritious foods than what kings had available to them only a few generations ago, and that's thanks to cold storage and transport, not healthcare.

Modern 'healthcare' claims credit for many improvements it did not contribute to. The thanks actually goes to economics (leading to greater wealth and being able to afford greater healthcare), engineering, transport, and agriculture.

Let me further clarify by splitting healthcare in two. There is emergency trauma care—what you'll get after a car crash—and there's 'disease care,' which gives you pills or dietary or lifestyle recommendations.

Those are both considered part of our medical system, but they could not be more different from each other.

I'll gladly concede that modern trauma care borders on the miraculous. Not long ago people died from infections from a rose thorn grazing their skin, yet somehow today someone can lose legs in a car crash, be blasted in a drive-by shooting, or suffer a sudden and catastrophic brain bleed... and if trauma care is applied quickly enough they can not only live but actually make a full recovery, perhaps minus a few body parts and with a few gnarly scars.

It's miraculous and I'm grateful for it. Were it not for modern medicine my wife and my firstborn child would both have died on what is in reality, thanks to modern medicine, the joyous occasion of my son's birthday.

Because I live now and not a few hundred years ago we joyfully celebrate a happy birthday every year as a family, whereas had the same events unfolded even just two hundred years ago it would be just me commemorating a lonely day of mourning for a lost wife and son.

In no way do I for a moment diminish the extraordinary achievements of modern medicine in trauma care. What it can do is borderline miraculous.

This medical technology is the product of amazing men and women following God's instruction to work hard and create value for others. These were *good* men and women who obeyed God's instruction to leave an inheritance to their children's children, in their case the inheritance was in the form of medical technology.

It is because of them that we benefit from generations of hard-won knowledge in medicine, biology, materials science, and so much more.

That's the 'trauma care' side of medicine, however 'disease care' is a very different reality.

Our ability to correctly diagnose disease has improved exponentially throughout the years, however, with some exceptions (which I'm grateful for), our ability to prevent, treat, and medicate disease remains limited at best, and *counterproductive* in many cases.

For the last sixty years governments have injected themselves ever more into disease care (pun fully intended). From the US 'Centre of Disease Control' to the Food and Drug Administration to the Australian Therapeutic Goods Administration and various equivalents around the world, there is a presumption that a medicine or healthcare protocol is only trustworthy, only 'safe and effective' if it has a stamp of approval from a bureaucrat.

If it doesn't have the stamp of approval from a government-funded or government-approved alphabet agency it is immediately suspect and will probably kill you... and of course, if something *does* have that stamp of approval then how dare you question whether it's safe or effective!

This is not only naïve, it's dangerous. The third-largest cause of death in the USA is medical malpractice, and most of that is due to 'approved' doctors wrongly prescribing 'approved' medications.

The idea that government approval makes something safe is naïve, but the idea that a *lack* of government approval makes it *dangerous* is idolatry.

Yet even as the bodies from medical malpractice and 'approved' drugs stack up to heaven, the devastating effect of government intervention in disease care is masked by ever-improving engineering and technology which has been extending life expectancy and wellbeing *in spite* of the government.

Again, the government is claiming credit for things it did not do. The improvements in life-expectancy, wellbeing, and trauma care came from people obeying God's design and leaving an inheritance in the form of engineering, infrastructure, knowledge, and technology.

Government deserves the credit for none of those things, but they take the credit anyway. They deceive us by claiming *they* did that, and then they claim they should be trusted, obeyed, even venerated for it.

They say, "How *dare* you suggest the food pyramid isn't the gospel truth! The food pyramid was published by experts and we know they're experts because they have the government approved credentials to say so!"

So you *have to believe them* despite the fact they can't decide if butter or margarine is better this year, or whether more than two eggs a day will save your life with wonderful nutrition or kill you with runaway cholesterol... and despite the fact that since the publishing of the food pyramid the USA and the Western World in general have become more and more obese and lifestyle- and diet-related diseases have become increasingly prominent... You *have* to believe them, because they're the experts! And you *know* they're the experts because the government said so!

How *dare* you ask if SSRIs, which inhibit the uptake of serotonin, leading to higher levels of serotonin in the blood where it gets measured (so it looks good in tests) but further reduces the amount of serotonin received in the brain where it's needed (deepening depression and contributing to terrible side-effects including suicidal thoughts) is actually a good idea!

What could you possibly know that the government approved *experts* don't?

How *dare* you wonder if statins or low-cholesterol diets are actually a good idea given that our brains are mostly *made* of cholesterol and doctor-prescribed low-cholesterol diets have risen in correlation with dementia rates?

How *dare you!*

Now, some will object that of *course* the official advice is always changing, because science and research leads to new discoveries and improved knowledge.

But notice how this new science and research always has to come from government-approved and usually government-funded bodies? Notice how questioning the official advice is *heresy* until the officials change the advice themselves?

Notice how *you* aren't allowed to notice that they're wrong before *they* tell you?

And even when they admit they were wrong they don't so much admit they were *wrong*... it's just that new research has uncovered new information that they couldn't *possibly* have known before... even if lots of other people did...

This is not open inquiry and science befitting a post-enlightenment world. It's a new priesthood with lab coats as their robes, test tubes as their rites, and peer reviewed journals as their ever-changing bible.

The problem is not the science and research. That's a great thing and is exactly what God would have us do!

The problem is the *veneration* of 'science' and the unquestioning obedience that is demanded of us. The problem is the idolatry of Government-Rapha.

You may think I'm overly cynical, but once again let's put this to the test. If this is idolatry, a new religion, Satan's perversion of God's created design, then it will have terrible outcomes. Satan comes to steal, kill, and destroy. His perversion of God's design will always lead to those outcomes, so health will be no exception.

And it turns out that Government-Rapha, government-our-healer and the perversion of 'disease care,' is stealing, killing, and destroying us, *literally.*

I'm sorry to report that the ongoing improvement in wellbeing and lifespan seen over the last few hundred years, driven largely by engineering and sanitation and a little by medicine, appears to have peaked.

Life expectancy increases have slowed for the first time in centuries (excluding the effect of wars), and record numbers of people are getting sicker, younger... and the *government* is directly responsible for an unfolding tragedy.

Sounds over-dramatic? Let me explain.

For decades the government's 'tick of approval' has been the gold-standard in healthcare. There have been approval schemes for every drug or therapy and government registration required for every medical professional, and in most countries, making 'non-approved' claims about a medicine or therapy or practising any medical discipline without the government's approval would lead to deregistration, fines, or prison.

Governments created their own agencies and bureaucracies to oversee these approval processes but the problem is that, as we'll continue to see, governments frequently accomplish the opposite of what they set out to achieve.

For example the food pyramid has been pushed by governments around the world as the gold standard in dietary 'balance,' but its introduction has coincided with a many-fold increase in obesity, heart disease, diabetes, dementia, and more, everywhere it's been adopted. While parts of the world that continued their traditional 'unhealthy' diets have been largely unaffected.

Coincidence? Are people in Western countries obese because they've ignored the government's 'health' advice, or because they've followed it?

In a world where sugary breakfast cereals are given a better 'health rating' than apples, you know the answer.

The breakfasts we used to eat in the 1950s, before the government started making 'recommendations,' were healthier than the breakfasts most of us eat now. Eggs and steak, perhaps with bacon, fried buttery mushrooms, and spinach or tomato, will always be healthier than most cereals no matter what the food pyramid says.

Look at the ever-changing advice on how many eggs is safe to eat, or the flip-flopping between whether butter or margarine is better.

Fat was demonised for a few decades, aided by government agencies and big-budget, government-funded 'research' (more on that later), and so 'low fat' food became the 'healthy choice.'

But low fat often means low flavour, and to compensate our food became high sugar! Obesity exploded, along with the profits of processed food companies, and now of course it's sugar that is being demonised! I agree that sugar is a huge problem, but it only became a problem because the government incorrectly demonised fat, which we're now 'discovering' isn't so bad after all!

These are just a few examples of far too many. Medical 'science' is held as some sort of sacred text, and if you were to question it or, heaven forbid, 'do your own research' on any topic then you're an idiot who should shut up and 'trust the experts.'

Nowhere is this more true than with 'double-blind placebo-controlled studies.' If someone can say 'studies have shown' then they're assumed to be absolutely 100% correct...

...never mind that there's a 'replication' crisis going on as researchers are unable to get the same results when they repeat decades-old, seemingly rock-solid 'double-blind, placebo-controlled' studies.

This becomes concerning when you realise that researchers and regulators often rely on these old 'rock-solid' studies in their work, and if half of them can't be replicated... what kind of foundation is this new work being built on?

And never mind that more than ten thousand medical studies were withdrawn in 2023 alone and those ten thousand retractions are only the tip of the iceberg.

According to Ivan Oransky and Adam Marcus from Retraction Watch, which is the most authoritative source for such information, there should be at least 100,000 retractions a year, with the real extent of the problem unknown and unknowable at this time.

And this is just from *new* studies each year. If there's at *least* 100,000 new studies every year which *should* be withdrawn then what's the cumulative total of existing studies from the last fifty years which should *also* be withdrawn but are instead accepted as gospel fact?

Millions? Tens of millions? How many good and decent people have dedicated their lives to medical science research, not realising that the foundation they are trying to build on is flawed or even fraudulent?

We cannot know.

There are decades-old studies which have been cited in new research thousands of times, and yet they cannot be replicated when researchers try. These studies are treated as 'gospel truth' but they're actually fraud.

And this is the 'god' we worship. This is your 'Government-Rapha.'

The combination of honest mistakes, flaws in methodology, publish-or-perish pressure, funding expectations, career ambitions, and good old fashioned fraud for profit, is a toxic mix, and sadly much of what is considered to be 'gospel' in our newly-formed idol of 'science,' and especially medical science, is actually nonsense.

To be clear, I'm not saying that *everything* we think we know is wrong, but a *lot* is, and we don't yet know with confidence which is which.

We don't know what we don't know, yet we're increasingly being required to 'trust the science' and pretend that ordinary people like you and I are not capable of doing our own research and discerning for ourselves what is wisdom and what is likely to be nonsense when it comes to medicine.

But a healthy scepticism is flooding the public consciousness. The white-gowned high priests of medical scientism are no longer considered infallible, and I for one am delighted.

For example, high protein, high fat, low carb diets are being adopted by millions, myself included. I'm eating more fat than ever before in my life, and so far I've lost 15kg (over 33lb!) and I'm not done losing weight yet. Best of all, that weight loss and the accompanying improvement in my energy levels, mental clarity, and general wellbeing has felt effortless. I'm not 'on a diet' and I don't feel hungry, I've simply made a sustainable lifestyle change which I'm quite enjoying, contrary to my past efforts to lose weight by following the official 'diet' recommendations.

Rejecting the government-approved food pyramid has had a wonderful *positive* effect on my health, and there are millions like me. As a result of this and other factors there's a rapidly growing realisation that, contrary to popular belief for the last fifty years, the government really doesn't know what it's talking about when it comes to health.

Sacred cows of modern medicine such as low-fat, low-salt, and low-cholesterol diets are now being legitimately questioned, with rapidly-growing counter-cultural movements pushing back against the official 'wisdom.'

Even absolutely rock-solid unquestionable medical 'facts' like 'the sun is bad for you' with its government-funded 'slip, slop, slap' message from my childhood in Australia is now suspect! Tens of millions of dollars has been spent over my lifetime urging people to cover up from the sun and billions has been spent on cancer research... yet in my lifetime the skin cancer rates in Australia have doubled, not decreased.

Men used to work shirtless all the time but now worksites mandate full body coverings and hats. Kids once played in just shorts in the full sun, and going outside to 'get some sun' was enforced by parents on kids all through summer and winter. Now they go out with UV rated clothing and hats with flaps to protect the neck, lathered in chemical-based sunscreens. Weekend cricket matches or BBQs used to be populated by shirtless or short-sleeved men who now cover up in compliance with the multi-million-dollar government-funded slip-slop-slap campaign.

The government got what it wanted, we obeyed our 'Government-Rapha,' and yet Cancer Australia reports that skin cancer rates have doubled in my lifetime.

Wasn't the science settled? Weren't the high priests infallible? Less sun was *sure* to lead to less skin cancer...

So why didn't it?

People are beginning to notice that the promises of Government-Rapha never seem to come true, and they're beginning to ask questions.

For example, the terrible effects of some sunscreen lotions are now well understood, and the fact that some sunscreens are actually carcinogenic is a darkly ironic twist in the tale. Plus the ravages of vitamin D deficiency, due in part to people over-protecting themselves from the sun, are starting to become apparent and this vitamin D deficiency has made some people more vulnerable to other illnesses, especially respiratory viruses.

The link between sun and skin-cancer *was* about as close to 'settled medical science' as you can get, yet after decades of relentless 'public awareness' campaigns the whole premise is coming into question and many people, myself included, are deliberately getting more sun on a regular basis and enjoying improved mood and improved health.

Cholesterol itself is a whole topic that is beyond the scope of this book, but the idea that dementia is actually 'type 3 diabetes' is now being seriously discussed among medical professionals, and the fact that our bodies *need* cholesterol as a building block of the brain is finally being recognised after decades of low-cholesterol diets just happening to coincide with record-breaking levels of dementia...

And speaking of coincidences, there's been a lot of 'died suddenly' headlines in the last few years... and people are noticing.

It's like a dam has burst and everywhere we look we can see the official 'health' advice being questioned or even just collapsing completely, and it's happening now because of the greatest 'disease care' crime in history: the Covid-19 saga.

The God of Covid

The emergence of the SARS CoV2 Coronavirus commonly known as Covid-19 onto a fearful post-faith Western culture was the perfect opportunity for governments around the world to step fully into their self-appointed role as god, as our Government-Nissi, our protector, and as Government-Rapha, our healer.

Western governments stepped up to the plate claiming god-like knowledge and god-like power to protect, to heal, to provide, and to guide. We, the little people who lacked this wisdom and power, simply *had* to accept that our government would manage and dictate every single aspect of our lives *and* we had to do exactly what we were told. If we did that then everything would work out just fine.

In my home city of Melbourne, Australia, being 'protected' by our Government-Nissi meant accepting and celebrating a totalitarian takeover of our lives, 'for our own good.'

In 2020 and 2021 we had the harshest and most far-reaching lockdown restrictions anywhere on earth, including:

- All 'non-essential' workers being banned from working. News-flash, every worker is essential to their family, their business, and to God's created order in which He provides for us through our work and trade.
- Defacto house arrest for twenty-three hours per day. If you weren't an 'essential worker' then you could leave your house *only* for a maximum of one hour per day, and only for an approved purpose, specifically:

  - Essential shopping for essential items only. We had shops fencing off some parts of their store to keep you away from 'non-essential items,' and police inspecting people's shopping bags to ensure they had only been purchasing 'essential' items!
  - Essential healthcare. Most healthcare was unavailable during Covid, and many millions of cancer screenings and other routine medical checkups were missed because the entire medical industry was conscripted to 'fight Covid' and Covid only.
  - Exercise, but only for one hour, within five kilometres of your home, and you had to be actively exercising. Police fined and arrested people for going on a walk and then stopping to sit on a park bench. Even elderly people were shown no mercy, fined or even arrested for sitting in the sun during their one hour of 'yard time.'
  - Essential caregiving, including shopping, for a person who couldn't do it for themselves.
- A five kilometre (three mile) perimeter. You were not permitted to travel further than that from your home. Police and Sheriff departments set up cameras to read car number plates and would pull you over if you were 'too far' from your registered address.
- A so-called 'ring of steel,' being a series of checkpoints cutting off the city of Melbourne from the rest of the

state of Victoria and locking 4.5 million people into the urban city. Uniformed military and police manned those checkpoints, unironically demanding to see 'papers please' if you wanted to pass through.

- An 8PM curfew, which was ruthlessly enforced, including some people being fined for the 'crime' of taking their bins out to the kerb after 8PM and one instance of someone being shot at by a police officer as they tried to drive away from being arrested for breaking curfew.
- No visitors to your home. People were actively encouraged to 'dob in' their neighbours if they had guests or if there were too many cars in the street.
- Schools were closed and parents had to home school, but *not* the good kind of home schooling! This simply made children sit in group video calls with their teacher and classmates for hours on end doing bookwork while losing their minds and driving their parents insane. It turned homes into pressure cookers and led to a spike in abuse, divorce, and mental breakdowns among young and old alike.
- Playgrounds and parks were closed. We had construction tape wrapped around children's playgrounds, tying up swings and blocking slides. Truckloads of sand and concrete bollards were deployed to make skate parks unusable and police patrolled beaches and parks to ensure no one stopped to just enjoy the fresh air and the view. I was one of a few people who cut the tape, freed the swings, and took my

children to play almost every day in defiance of the fearmongers.

- All gathering places were closed including pubs and bars, clubs, cinemas, and sporting events.
- The national border was shut down, stranding tens of thousands of Australians overseas, often in desperate situations, far from home, running out of money, and having to deal with whatever local lockdowns occurred where they were stranded. This was a complete betrayal of their citizenship.
- And the greatest crime of all: churches, mosques, and synagogues were all closed, and any pastors or rabbis who dared to gather and worship God on their appointed day were arrested and prosecuted.

All this and more in the 'free' country of Australia. These restrictions existed in one form or another foreighteenmonths.

The above is just the 'non-medical interventions.' It gets worse once you look at the medical side as well.

No sooner had the effectiveness of Hydroxychloroquine and Ivermectin (both in their appropriate therapeutic doses and pairings) been discovered than they were banned in Australia.

Imports of Ivermectin were blocked and confiscated, a huge shipment of Hydroxychloroquine, enough to help protect the entire country, which was purchased by Australian billionaire Clive Palmer and donated to the government for the public good, was seized and destroyed by the government, who were actively and mendaciously suppressing effective medical treatments in favour of lockdowns and an as-yet-undeveloped vaccine.

A globally coordinated misinformation campaign disparaged Ivermectin as dangerous, as 'horse paste,' and as ineffective. Yet even the doubters must now admit that Ivermectin works, as it is now included in the government-authorised therapies for Covid-19 in multiple countries.

Off-label prescription of both medicines was banned in Australia, making it an offence for any doctor to prescribe them for Covid and empowering the Australian Health Practitioner Regulation Agency (the agency that was supposed to 'keep us safe,' our Government-Nissi) to suspend the registration of doctors who committed the 'crime' of providing the best healthcare they could based on their best understanding of the medical options at the time.

This meant that when the mRNA jabs were released after their hurried development and limited testing they were eligible to be given an 'emergency use authorisation' by the Therapeutic Goods Administration.

It's important to note that this emergency use authorisation could *not* have been given for the mRNA jabs if there was an alternative... such as Ivermectin.

So the demonisation of proven safe and effective medications such as Ivermectin and Hydroxychloroquine, including the suspension of doctors who disobeyed the bans on off-label prescription, were a necessary prerequisite for the government to authorise the use of the mRNA jabs with their unknown safety profile and unproven effectiveness.

The Australian Government literally turned its regulatory regime which was supposed to 'keep us safe' from rogue medical operators (Government-Nissi) and bring us healing (Government-Rapha) into a weapon which denied the Australian people proven medical care and forced us to participate in the 'world's largest clinical trial,' as our then-Health Minister, Greg Hunt, called it.

You may have noticed that I refer to the mRNA jabs as 'jabs' and not as vaccines. There's a good reason I do this. There's a distinction between vaccines and these jabs, these gene therapies, which is very clear in the literature but is not yet well understood publicly.

Vaccines historically have been live-attenuated vaccines, or 'killed' vaccines, or fragments of vaccines, with variations within these categories. In all these types of vaccines the thing that is injected into the body is a controlled dose of a specific substance which the immune system then responds directly to, developing immunity.

The mRNA jabs add another crucial step which, in my opinion, means the 'vaccine' label no longer applies and we need to find a new label.

By design, mRNA jabs do not inject the thing the immune system is supposed to react to, they inject instructions for the body to *manufacture* that thing—in this case, spike proteins—and once the body manufactures it the immune system in your body responds and fights... itself.

This is a vitally important change, but its implications are not well appreciated by the general public! Because each person's body will respond differently due to natural variations in our physiology and we will each manufacture different quantities of spike proteins, meaning the 'dose' is wildly different from person to person.

It's also well established now that these spike proteins travel throughout the body and gather in vital organs in alarming concentrations, whereas typical vaccines usually stay at the injection site.

There are many more differences as well, but this distinction between a vaccine which injects a known quantity of foreign material into a specific site for the body to respond to and a jab which injects the *instructions* for the body to then *manufacture* the foreign material, and spreads it all over the body, is both vital and under-appreciated, and so I refuse to refer to the mRNA jabs as 'vaccines.'

This book is not about the medical specifics, though, so let's bring this back to government and idolatry.

The mRNA jabs were new and thus lacked long-term safety data. Further, the manufacturers were granted immunity (by our governments) from any adverse events, including deaths, that could occur, *and* the manufacturers were permitted to keep their research and trial data (what little there was) secret from the public. Meanwhile, the government mandated these new, untested jabs for people who wanted or needed to work, travel, play, or worship.

This is the government playing god with our bodies. "Trust us, you don't need to know, you just need to obey."

Once the mRNA jabs were approved under various governments' 'emergency use authorisations,' the level of human rights abuse in Australia and elsewhere went completely off the scale.

- All workers were mandated to *have* to take these untested jabs or lose their jobs.
- Workers who refused were either suspended without pay or dishonourably discharged. This included many police, nurses, doctors, teachers, and more.
- For everyone, your ability to attend church, go to sporting events, dine in restaurants, or even to visit friends and family, was made contingent on you having the jab.
- 'Covid Passports' became the norm, with people having to provide proof of vaccination or be denied entry. This is genuine medical apartheid.
- Even once the legal restrictions ended there continued to be an overwhelming 'public awareness' campaign aimed at persuading families to reject any members who were not jabbed from attending Christmas or other family gatherings.

And all of this was done to 'protect' us from a virus... which was the product of *mankind playing god* in the first place. Covid-19 was a man-made virus created through gain-of-function research which was funded by US taxpayers via the National Institutes of Health under the laughable 'oversight' of Anthony Fauci and carried out in the Wuhan lab because Fauci had been forced to move his gain-of-function work offshore from the US because it was considered too dangerous following leaks from US-based labs.

This is well documented in books such as *The Real Anthony Fauci* by Robert F. Kennedy, Jr.

Let's take stock of this grim scene and survey the facts as they are known today—and I mean only the non-controversial facts which are now (belatedly) accepted in the main-stream. Without any 'conspiracy' nonsense to muddy the waters, because this is one of the most perfect examples you will ever see of the 'Hegelian Dialectic,' of 'Problem, reaction, solution.'

The known and agreed facts are:

- Mankind played god with gain-of-function research on a virus, which either escaped by accident or intentionally, depending on who you believe. [Problem]
- In fear of that virus we then allowed government to play god and take total control over our daily lives, including our rights to leave home, work, play, and worship, to 'protect' us, and to ban medications it deemed to be the 'wrong' ones. [Reaction]
- In order to get out of those lockdowns we allowed government to play god with our bodies, the temples of the Holy Spirit, denying us proven medicines and coercing many into taking an unproved jab in return for their 'freedoms'... freedoms the government never had a right to take away in the first place. [Solution]

The idea of the Hegelian Dialectic is that the solution has already been decided by the powers that be, and the 'Problem' and the 'Reaction' are simply contrivances to convince the people to welcome the 'Solution' which has already been pre-determined.

This may sound far fetched, but consider:

- The problem of Covid was entirely man-made, whether released on purpose or by accident;
- The reaction of the media and political class was entirely predictable and largely driven by governments who got exactly the messaging they wanted; and the reaction of our medical regulators put us in a no-win situation where we were denied effective medical care and forced to 'wait' for the 'vaccines.'
- Arguably, both the problem and the reaction were simply contrivances designed to lead to the final destination of the solution: government mandated mRNA 'vaccines' which have now been taken by billions of people world-wide and have already impacted life expectancy and contributed to the ongoing precipitous drop in fertility, accelerating us rapidly towards a global population collapse.

Yes that last paragraph is a lot. You may find yourself instinctively trying to dismiss it, and perhaps this entire book with it, as a wild and speculative conspiracy theory.

I urge you not to look away just yet. Hold it in your mind as a possibility, even if only a remote one, for just a little longer. Keep it as an open possibility until you're read the rest of this book, and especially keep your mind open until you've read the chapter 'A Clash of World Views.'

The bottom line is this: The end result of the government playing god with our healthcare and our lives during Covid is that we are now watching the unfolding of the greatest healthcare disaster in history.

Worse than any of the World Wars.

Depending on how attentive you've been in the last few years, this claim of loss of life may already be obvious and accepted by you, or it may be the first you've heard of it, and perhaps you even remain convinced that mRNA jabs saved millions of lives from death by Covid.

If you're the latter then I urge you to read publications such as *Too Many Dead* by the Australian Medical Professionals Society and take a look at the all-cause mortality statistics for the country you live in. If it's anything like Australia, the total number of deaths will be running high since 2021. In Australia the excess deaths since the jab rollout have exceeded even the worst of Covid and have reversed a long-term trend of falling death rates and increasing average age of death, to now increasing death rates and falling life expectancy for some demographics, at least temporarily.

There is, of course, a great deal of debate about the exact cause for this excess death, but the fact that this excess is happening is beyond doubt in countries such as Australia with good statistics.

And whilst not every excess death is due to the jabs specifically, with many being attributable to things like missed cancer screenings due to lockdowns, the fact is that the mass injection of a novel and under-tested medical technology which just so happens to coincide with a rapid increase in mortality and decrease in life expectancy begs many questions.

Before you dismiss these excess deaths as the result of Covid or the dreaded and much-publicised 'Long Covid,' consider the data directly from Western Australia.

What makes Western Australia unique is that they took a 'fortress' approach to Covid and they kept Covid out of their state almost entirely until *after* large-scale mRNA jabs were administered there. In other words, they accidentally made themselves the *control group* in this global medical trial.

According to official Western Australian Government data there was an extraordinary rise in adverse events following vaccination, these are medical events and hospitalisations which cannot be explained by Covid infection.

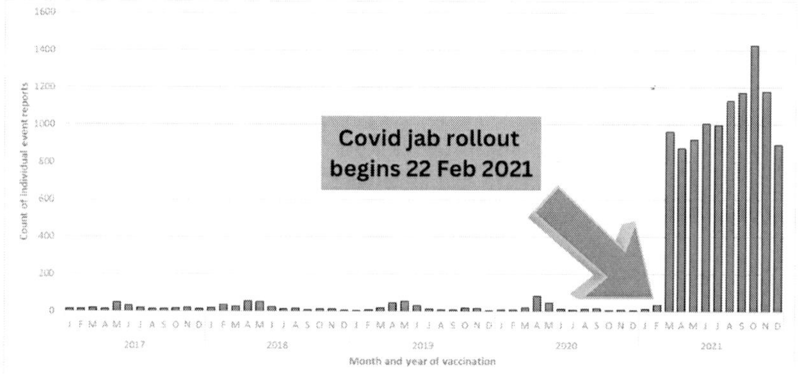

Figure 2: Adverse events following immunisation reported to WAVSS by month, 2017-2021, excluding active surveillance reports for routine vaccination adverse events.

Western Australian Vaccine Safety Surveillance – Annual Report 2021

The rate of adverse events from these mRNA vaccines was up more than twenty-three *times* the rate of adverse events from other vaccines:

Table 14: Numbers of vaccines administered, and adverse events reported, with rate of adverse events, for non COVID-19 vaccines and COVID-19 vaccines, 2021.

Vaccine type	Number of vaccines administered in 2021	Number of adverse events reported to WAVSS	Rate of adverse events per 100,000 doses
Non COVID-19	1,808,050	200	11.1
COVID-19	3,948,673	10,428	264.1

x 23.8

Western Australian Vaccine Safety Surveillance – Annual Report 2021

This is about as clear a 'smoking gun' as you'll ever get in the real world. Covid could *not* be the cause of these reactions and hospitalisations that started spiking in Western Australia *before* Covid was in the community, indicating that Covid is also *not* the cause elsewhere in the world, even in places where Covid did come before the jabs.

So if it's not Long Covid then what is the culprit for this unprecedented world-wide loss of life which our governments seem so incurious about?

For Western Australia, the Hermit Kingdom with hard border closures for two years, there is only one thing that changed at the same time as the reactions and deaths began to spike.

The jab rollout began.

And given that it was the jabs that caused the spike in deaths in Western Australia, then it was also the jabs that caused the excess deaths after 2020 everywhere else as well.

The full extent of this tragedy is unknown because it is still unfolding in real time before our eyes as I write this.

The wave of sudden deaths among the newly jabbed was so significant that the media couldn't ignore it and invented the term 'Sudden Adult Death Syndrome.'

As the saying goes, there is none so blind as one who *will* not see.

The mRNA jab rollout was accompanied by an epidemic of 'died suddenly' headlines, catalogued extensively in Edward Dowd's book *Cause Unknown*. There's excess deaths worldwide, as catalogued by the Australian Medical Professionals Society's report *Too Many Dead*.

But it's not over yet.

Whilst very few people are lining up for more mRNA booster jabs meaning that the worst of the heart failures have probably already happened and those waves of 'sudden' and 'unexplained' deaths are finally waning, a new phenomenon is rising fast to take their place: turbo cancer.

That's not the medical term of course, but it's the term that those who have been paying attention, including many doctors, have given to the sudden rise in hyper-aggressive cancers in those who have received the mRNA jabs. These 'turbo cancers' seem to appear out of nowhere with people's first diagnosis being for 'stage 4' cancer, and in some cases people can be dead within weeks.

This wasn't completely unheard of previously, but the numbers now are astonishing. *Something* has changed.

What changed was that the government *helped* us. It *saved* us. It was our Government-Rapha, our healer, and our Government-Nissi, our refuge, against a 'one in one hundred year pandemic,' which, it turned out, was less deadly than at least two other flus we've seen in the last one hundred years...

and where tragically the 'medicine' is proving to be deadlier than the disease.

The Asian Flu pandemic of 1957-58 killed between one and four million people worldwide, with a global population only one third of today's. That would be like a death toll of three to twelve million people today, which makes it on-par with Covid-19, which has an official death toll of seven million people over four years at the time of writing.

Keep in mind that this Covid-19 death toll is known to be wildly exaggerated, thanks to many people who died *with* Covid having been categorised as dying *of* Covid due to financial incentives and social or professional pressure.

I love the joke: "Did you hear about the pilot who crashed into a mountain in 2020? He died of Covid."

Covid deaths have been greatly exaggerated, and yet at the time of writing Covid-19 has accounted for barely 3% of global deaths since its emergence, which is almost exactly what you'd expect, given that on average approximately 3.2% of all deaths globally tend to be from influenza and related respiratory ailments.

So no, Covid-19 was no one in one hundred year killer, and there's an argument to be made that when you consider that the regular cold and flu 'disappeared' during Covid, and that 3% or more of all deaths in a year are normally caused by influenza, there's a compelling argument to be made that it doesn't even qualify as a 'bad' flu... just as a 'flu.'

Then there's the Hong Kong Flu pandemic of 1968-69 which is estimated to have killed between 1 and 4 million people, translating to between 2.5 and 10 million people when adjusted for today's population.

And this is to say nothing of the Spanish Flu which happened almost exactly one hundred years prior to Covid-19 and took place in a world with a population well under two billion people, yet still killed approximately 25 million souls. Adjusted for today's population that would be over 100 million people dead. *That* is what a real one in one hundred year pandemic looks like. Covid-19? It was just a flu, *maybe* a bad flu, and certainly nothing more than that. We'll see another flu like it within a few decades, guaranteed.

So why was the reaction from government so different this time given this flu was, relatively speaking, run of the mill?

Why, indeed.

What has changed between the 1950s and 60s and now that would cause something as unremarkable as a flu to be blown up into a once-in-a-lifetime 'war' requiring martial law, conscription into medical experiments, and human rights abuses normally reserved for the third world?

What changed? Government changed.

Government changed from being our servant, well aware of the limits of its power, to being our master and believing that *nothing* is outside its power.

Since the 1960s, government has become god.

And we are largely to blame. Today we look to the government for a solution to every little thing, and we certainly looked to the government to 'save' us from the dreaded Covid-19! And when we ask politicians to take the place of god, they are only too happy to oblige.

I discuss the perverse incentives of politics in detail in my first book, Good People Break Bad Laws, and I won't repeat myself here except to say that politicians are rewarded for 'doing something' even if that 'something' turns out to be ineffective or even bad. When people cry out to a politician to 'do something,' the politician will willingly oblige even if they have no idea what they're doing, and the unfolding disaster we see before us is the inevitable result.

Government-controlled 'disease care' is now directly responsible for the worst world health disaster in history. Government played god in a perfect Hegelian Dialectic, from the 'problem' of gain-of-function research gone wrong (or right, if you're a little more conspiratorial), to the 'reaction' of banning Ivermectin- and Hydroxychloroquine-based therapies and imposing draconian lockdowns awaiting a miracle 'vaccine' to be developed in record time, to the 'solution' of mandatory experimental mRNA jabs, which made pharmaceutical companies many billions of dollars at taxpayers' expense and have led directly to an unfolding health crisis of historic proportions.

Health is being destroyed, in the name of health, thanks to our government healthcare... our Goverment-Rapha.

And when you understand how government works, you realise that such an adverse outcome isn't a surprise. It's inevitable.

It isn't a bug of 'the system,' it's a feature.

It's what happens every time you replace our true God with an idol, Jehovah Rapha with government healthcare.

Reality Check

One of the challenges of writing a book is that it will be read by *very* different people with very different world views.

You may have read the last chapter and thought, *"Yes, finally, someone is saying it!"* or you might have read the last chapter and thought, "What a kook!"

...And I have to allow for both.

So just in case, I think it's time for us to have an honest look at ourselves and our freedoms—a reality check. We need to consider whether we're as free as we tell ourselves, even putting the Covid era to one side for a moment.

One of many unfortunate human failings is that our perceptions are usually formed by a combination of what we've been told by others in our childhood and what we've observed ourselves over the years since. And once an opinion is formed it is usually slow to change. This means that our perceptions often lag behind the reality of life around us, usually by years or even decades.

If I ask an average American, "Is America a free country?" most will quickly say "Yes," and might even insist that it's the freest country on earth!

They'll cite the War of Independence and Independence Day, the Bill of Rights, and the fact that America is 'fighting for freedom' all over the world as proof they're correct.

I'd say those things are proof that they *were* correct... but they stopped being correct about seventy years ago.

Putting an exact date on when the USA, or any other part of the Western world, ceased to be free is impossible. It was a gradual process.

The creation of the Federal Reserve System was a terrible blow to freedom in America. So was the Depression-era 'New Deal,' and countless other 'death by one thousand cuts'-style failings.

But whatever the exact date of its loss, a simple stocktake will quickly demonstrate that although the USA and other Western countries have many great features, freedom in any genuine sense is no longer one of them, except perhaps in comparison to other places which have never been free.

Let's take the US Bill of Rights as just one example. You don't have to agree or disagree with these first ten amendments to the US Constitution to recognise that almost none of them are still respected in any meaningful way.

You can exercise your First Amendment rights to freedom of speech... if you have pockets deep enough to fight a five-year legal battle up to the Supreme Court!

The Second Amendment right to bear arms? Today that's only for hunting and home defence, and if you want any of the 'militia'-worthy weapons which the Second Amendment specifically protected your right to own... well, thanks to the NFA you'd better go get extra government permission for that!

Again this isn't about whether or not you're pro-gun, it's about whether these constitutional 'rights' still mean anything in the land of the 'free.'

Fourth Amendment rights to be protected from warrantless searches are a joke in a country of stop-and-search, immigration patrols, roadside stops for any reason, and a hyper-aggressive and all-pervasive 'war on drugs.'

Fifth Amendment right to due process and compensation if your property is confiscated? Dream on. Civil asset forfeiture is legalised theft of the most brazen kind.

If you've never heard of 'civil asset forfeiture' you'd better look it up and prepare to have your mind blown. Police departments in many US States get to confiscate property which was in *any* way related to a crime, no matter how tenuous the link, and sell that property, and then that police department gets to *keep the money.*

US citizens have literally had their houses seized and sold because a suspected drug dealer ran *through* their property whilst attempting to evade capture. Yes, you read that right. That's happening right now in the 'free' old US of A.

The Sixth Amendment giving you the right to a speedy trial with an unbiased jury? Again, not anymore. "Justice delayed is justice denied," said William E. Gladstone in the 1800s, a sentiment echoed by Martin Luther King Jr., among others, and yet US citizens languish in prisons awaiting trial for months and years, and when they get to trial they find that judges often 'instruct' juries in ways which completely compromise their independence and therefore justice, meaning the only pathway to justice is more delays and money in appeals.

Do I need to go on?

The Bill of Rights has teeth only for those rich enough to back it up with an army of lawyers. It is, in the end, just words on a page. Most people do not have the resources to hold the government accountable when it breaches their rights, and the US Government uses that to its advantage.

But at least the Bill of Rights exists! In countries which have relied on Common (historic) law rather than an explicit bill of rights the situation is so much worse.

In the UK we're seeing people arrested and imprisoned for Facebook posts, in Canada we saw people losing drivers licenses and truck registrations for peacefully protesting against the government border lockdowns during Covid, and in Australia I'm one of numerous people who lost years of our lives and tens of thousands of dollars fighting *criminal* charges because I encouraged people to speak up and show up to peaceful protests against the most overbearing Covid lockdowns on earth in Melbourne, Australia.

In many parts of the 'enlightened' Western world you can be imprisoned or at least fined stupendous amounts of money for objecting publicly *or* privately to irreversible transgender surgeries for children who aren't old enough to get a tattoo. Stating that marriage is between a man and a woman will bankrupt you in a hurry if the 'wrong' person takes offence, and meanwhile we're witnessing the rise of a State-controlled media so brazen that it would make the editors of Pravda blush.

And when it comes to wars, I think the last time the Western world truly fought for freedom was in WWII, and even elements of that weren't exactly a 'clean conscience' war for freedom! Witness the way the US and UK treated French Partisans who were Communists towards the end of the war... deceiving them into doomed missions against the retreating Germans, leading them as lambs to the slaughter for the specific purpose of killing them off in a preemptive strike against the looming cold war against the Communist regime of the USSR.

Now to be clear, war is always a terrible and messy business and I mean no offence to the soldiers on the ground who are sent by our government into those wars. Many or indeed most soldiers serve their countries to the best of their abilities and with the best of intentions in the most awful conditions. But the fact is that old men in suits are making wars for young men in uniform to die in, and those men in suits will tell whatever lies they must to get the young men to die willingly.

"Go and fight for freedom!" is a lie that works well. But ask a combat veteran from any of the wars in the last 40 years whether they really believe that was true, or whether that's what the 'suits' said to convince the 'uniforms' to go and die in a war that was really about anything *but* freedom.

I've asked many combat veterans that question, and less than half have said they still believe it was about freedom in any meaningful sense. Imagine having to live with that after all you've been through, after all the suffering you witnessed, and with the internal battles you're doomed to fight for the rest of your days... to have all that on your shoulders and not even be able to be certain you were sent there for the right reasons.

The motives of the Korean war were certainly less pure than WWII had been, but this conflict was still possibly defensible as a battle for freedom against the genuine tyrannical repression of Communism, and there is a silver lining in that the result of the war in the form of the separate North Korea and South Korea has given the world it's clearest possible object lesson in the benefits of Capitalism and the dangers of Communism.

But by the time you get to the Vietnam war with all the involvement of the CIA, rampant drug running, and the games being played in the background, it gets hard to claim it was a war for freedom. Profiteering was now a primary motivation for many of the suits behind the war, as well as rank politics. Freedom? Not so much.

The first war in Iraq was murky at best, and as for 'Iraq II - Return of the Bush,' it was built on a lie.

The invasion and occupation of Afghanistan was a humanitarian disaster at every level, enriching the military-industrial complex at the cost of lives and lifelong trauma for US and allied soldiers, as well as for many of the people of Afghanistan, and all we have to show for the expense, suffering, and death, is a total capitulation to Taliban rule and the abandonment of all those who had helped the US forces for twenty years.

Ukraine? It's a blood-for-money laundering scheme where politicians spend billions of the taxpayers dimes buying weapons from US military contracting companies which in turn lobby those same politicians, showering them with gifts, funding their campaigns, and giving them cushy board positions to retire on post-politics. Those weapons are used and destroyed immediately in a foreign country, spilling foreign blood, and only a few months later the cycle of taxpayer-funded back scratching starts all over again.

Fighting for freedom? The individual soldiers might be, but the suits sending those soldiers to war and signing the weapons contracts? Not by a long shot. They're feathering their nests, accumulating power, influence, and allies, and enriching themselves and their fellow travellers, all with devastating effects on the decent men and women they send to war, not to mention the countries the wars are fought in.

Former US President Dwight Eisenhower, notable for leading the D-Day Landings at Normandy and being the Supreme Commander of the Allied Expeditionary Forces in Europe, had much to say about the danger of what he called the 'military-industrial complex' in his farewell address in 1961.

This was six years in to the French-Vietnam war, but years before the US entered that war in 1965, and well before it became the full disaster that it was by the time the US pulled out in 1975:

"A vital element in keeping the peace is our military establishment. Our arms must be mighty, ready for instant action, so that no potential aggressor may be tempted to risk his own destruction...

"Our military organization today bears little relation to that known by any of my predecessors in peace time, or indeed by the fighting men of World War II or Korea.

"Until the latest of our world conflicts, the United States had no armaments industry... American makers of plowshares could, with time and as required, make swords as well. But now we can no longer risk emergency improvisation of national defence; we have been compelled to create a permanent armaments industry of vast proportions... Added to this, three and a half million men and women are directly engaged in the defense establishment. We annually spend on military security more than the net income of all United State corporation.

"This conjunction of an immense military establishment and a large arms industry is new in the American experience. The total influence, economic, political, even spiritual is felt in every city, every state house, every office of the Federal government. We recognise the imperative need for this development. Yet we must not fail to comprehend its grave implications. Our toil, resources and livelihood are all involved; so is the very structure of our society.

"In the councils of government, we must guard against the acquisition of unwarranted influence, whether sought or unsought, by the military-industrial complex. The potential for the disastrous rise of misplaced power exists and will persist.

"We must never let the weight of this combination endanger our liberties or democratic processes. We should take nothing for granted. Only an alert and knowledgeable citizenry can compel the proper meshing of the huge industrial and military machinery of defence with our peaceful methods and goals, so that security and liberty may prosper together."

More than sixty years later the prescience of his warning is clear, and the fact that we failed to heed it is tragic.

This change that has taken place since WWII is not some figment of my feverish imagination; it was called out by President Eisenhower, who had intimate inside knowledge both as a military commander and as the President. But we ignored him and most people's perception is still stuck in the past... in the 'justice' of the wars we fought before the 1950s, not in the reality of the wars we've fought since the 1970s.

The influence of the military-industrial complex on US policy, and indeed on the NATO alliance and the world, is now deeply entrenched and parasitic.

I believe it's fair to say that while we the people are guilty of idolatry for worshipping government, the government itself worships violence and, especially, worships war.

War has become a god, the worship of which is enabled by our over-mighty governments and the egomaniacs which occupy them, enabled by a parasitic military industrial complex that squanders lives to gather dollars, and it's happened on our watch and largely without our notice.

The trouble is that our perceptions of the world we live in were formed in our childhood by the opinions of grown-ups whose perceptions were formed in *their* childhood.

The opinions we are given in childhood are probably already out of date when they are passed to us by our parents, teachers, and elders, and those ideas are also slow to change as we age, meaning that unless we actually start paying attention our perceptions of the country we live in and the world around us could be fifty years old or more.

There's a saying, "It is easier to fool someone than it is to convince them they've been fooled." That's because once we form an opinion it's harder to change than it was to form in the first place.

I joined the military in Australia in the post 9-11 rush of patriotic young men who were keen to 'defend freedom' and fight the 'war on terror.'

I was young and delusional.

I was motivated by the best of intentions and a desire to do good, to help, to spread *freedom* to far-flung parts of the world where we would no doubt be welcomed as heroes and liberators and return home to ticker-tape parades just like 'the greatest generation' did at the end of WWII.

Of course, I grew up reading WWII history and that largely formed my idea of what war was. I believed that the Western world valued freedom above all else, and that if we were going to fight somewhere then it was *of course* a fight for freedom—and how dare you suggest otherwise!

To question the legitimacy of a war was to insult our troops and spit on their graves, a crime of blasphemy in my conservative upbringing. Yes the military can be an idol too.

I wanted nothing more than to deploy to a far-flung country and go and 'fight for freedom' against some oppressive tyrant somewhere. I'm embarrassed to say I was itching for it! And for a while I was frustrated that there really wasn't much opportunity to deploy with the Australian Infantry at that time.

Looking back I'm incredibly grateful that I never deployed to a warzone and never saw combat. I have enormous respect and empathy for those who did and I *know* that they did it for the right reasons, because I *know* that if my deployment had come then I would have done it for the 'right reasons' too, but that doesn't change the fact we were being used, and what we *did* would have been wrong, no matter how pure our intentions.

I consider my few years in the army my time seeing 'behind the curtain.' Just like how in *The Wizard of Oz*, Oz the Great and Terrible is revealed to be just a little man surrounded by pomp and ceremony and clever devices to make himself seem far more substantial than he really was, I found the military to be the same.

I was shocked at how 'human' it was. I saw people who would, if we deployed, be making life-and-death moral judgements in the heat of battle, yet they were acting with all the same moral failings you might expect from a self-important shift supervisor at a McDonald's.

After a few years grappling with what I was seeing I finally realised I'd been fooled. The military, this organisation that I'd been taught by my conservative upbringing to revere and support without question, was frail, human, in some ways rotten, and completely undeserving of the blind support I'd given it up to that point.

It took me years of 'seeing behind the curtain' to have that realisation, such is the power of an opinion, once formed.

The same is true of your opinion of the country where you live, and the government you have. You were told in your childhood that the English-speaking world was free, and you believed it, and unless something big happens (or has already happened) to shock you out of your current opinion then it's going to take a lot to change your mind.

It's another way of saying 'first impressions last,' and it's made worse by the innate 'confirmation bias' which we all suffer from.

Confirmation bias is simply the ability of the brain to see and hear what it wants and expects to hear based on your current beliefs, and to filter out the things that don't line up with those current beliefs.

The fact is, we're quite attached to the idea that we're free, and there's no question that we're certainly very comfortable, which makes it very tempting to turn a blind eye to any problems we may see… because observing those problems is a threat to our comfort…

Realising that we're *not* free, and thinking that maybe we need to *do* something about that, is very *un*comfortable. Such a view jeopardises our comfort, our lifestyle, and our social status, and calls us to take risks.

Believing that perhaps we are not so free after all conflicts with our current beliefs and opinions, but thankfully if we just allow our confirmation bias to 'do its thing' then we find ample evidence to support the idea that everything is just fine, we're free just like we've always believed, and you can go on living in the future exactly as you have done in the past with your bubble of comfort intact.

phew

But that's a lie. And if we don't stand up to reclaim our freedom today, while it's relatively easy, then we condemn our children to have to do it when it's much harder.

The truth is that the world is changing around us and becoming less free thanks to the worship of government, and to borrow the famous phrase from Benjamin Franklin, "*Those who would give up essential liberty to purchase a little temporary safety* [or comfort!] *deserve neither liberty nor safety*."

But confirmation bias isn't the only bias we have that works against us. The bias that politicians love to weaponise against us is a thing called 'normalcy bias.'

Normalcy bias is a form of confirmation bias which assumes that deviations from the 'norm' are exceptions, and that things will go back to 'normal' given a bit of time and trust.

Our normalcy bias is weaponised against us by politicians when they speak of 'emergency measures' and 'temporary measures.' They're saying, "We know you wouldn't *normally* agree to this, but these are *exceptional* circumstances. It's only *temporary*, and everything will go back to *normal.*"

Except that it doesn't.

Milton Freidman famously said, *"Nothing is so permanent as a temporary government program."*

For proof that he's right you need only look at something as simple as the income tax. It was introduced differently in different countries, but always either as a *temporary* wartime measure, or as something that will only affect the very, *very* wealthy. *I.e.*, it promised that *your* life would soon go back to *normal.* This wouldn't really affect *you.*

Yet, over one hundred years later, the 'wartime emergency' is over, the income tax hasn't been repealed anywhere, and it's now nearly universal and affects almost everyone.

Worse, it now feels *normal.* If you were to suggest getting rid of income tax you'd have a fight on your hands! Even the people that pay the tax would get mad at you for suggesting something that would upset their cosy little 'normal' lives.

"It's the price we pay to live in a civilised society!" they huffily object.

Actually, taxation is contrary to God's design and intention for government!

God instructed His people to bring a 10% tithe to the Church for the functioning of His temple, and He never instructed any taxes to fund the government *He* designed. Yes, God *allows* taxation and instructs us to pay taxes, but it wasn't *His* idea.

Recall that when the children of Israel demanded a king God explicitly and very strongly warned the children of Israel that the king will take 10% of everything, making them the kings slaves!

God literally equated 10% taxation with slavery. Today we have over 50% tax (if you add them all together) in pretty much every Western Country, and people will *fight* you if you tell them we need to reduce it.

I know they'll fight because I *have* told people we need to reduce our taxes and I *have* been attacked for it!

How did this become *normal*? How did we get to the point that our fellow 'free' citizens actually fight to *keep* their chains bound tightly around themselves?

The process is that politicians weaponise your normalcy bias to bring in 'emergency' 'temporary' measures, knowing that you would never ordinarily agree. They fool you with promises that everything will soon go back to 'normal,' and once enough time passes for these 'temporary' measures to *become* normal, it's that very same normalcy bias that will cause you to *defend* keeping the now-normal 'temporary' program you would have resisted in the first place!

The government has been able to grow from being our servant to being our god via one 'temporary' program after another. Because it was gradual, 'temporary,' and 'for your own good,' it all feels normal.

You've grown up being told that you're free, and that everything you see around you is *normal* and right and good.

That makes it very difficult to see clearly the abundant evidence that is all around us that our freedoms are rapidly fading and the world we're passing to our children is far less free than the one we were given.

Once you can see past your confirmation and normalcy biases you'll quickly recognise ample evidence of the way the world has changed all around you.

Today you must be careful what you say, be careful how 'Christian' you are in public, not disagree with the wrong people, and not support the wrong causes.

If you're in the 'wrong' industry (logging, mining, cattle ranching, or sheep exporting, to name a few), you'll live in fear of being shut down by the government without notice.

If you're a school counsellor or church pastor you need to always be on your guard not to say something that will get you into trouble—and you never know if it's going to be someone in your own congregation or one of your students' parents who will 'dob you in' for wrong-think.

The value you create through work and trade is confiscated from you by government taxes and wasted or handed out in return for little to no value, and you're the bad guy if you object. Thanks to government we no longer leave an inheritance to our children's children, but rather we're leaving debt with little to show for it.

You can be a Christian in the Western world today in the same way you can be a Christian in China: you can call yourself a 'Christian,' you can show up to a place called a 'church,' and you can say prayers to someone you call 'God'... but only the approved prayers, the approved church, and if you follow the approved doctrines about your god.

Yes, we're there, in the Western world, today.

This is not normal.

And don't ever let anyone ever tell you otherwise.

More to the point, this was not a part of God's design for government in the Old Testament, nor is this what God intended in the New Testament, or for us today.

The reality is, we are far closer to living in an oppressive dystopia than most of us realise. In many ways we're already there, and it's dangerous to allow your confirmation bias and desire for 'normalcy' to convince you otherwise.

The Promise of Heaven

Mankind have been trying to kill or become God since Satan lied to Eve and said she would 'become like God' if she ate fruit from the Tree of the Knowledge of Good and Evil.

The idea that humans can 'become like God' was alluring back then, and remains Satan's most powerful lie to this day.

And what better way to prove that you've become god, than for the government to create Heaven on Earth?

But just as Adam and Eve eating the forbidden fruit did *not* make us God, but rather separated us from God, so trying to create Heaven on Earth creates suffering and misery, taking us one step closer to hell.

The government doesn't always promise a full utopia, although sometimes it does, but the promise is always that the government will fix your problems, meet your needs, and make your life better. The promise is that the government is the *solution*, not the problem.

In the case of Communism, the promise *is* full utopia! Marx theorised it and the Bolshevik revolution tried to realise it in what had been Imperial Russia. The promise was that everything would belong to the people in common.

Private property, instituted by God in His design for how He would be our provider, was abolished, and all land, business, industry, titles, and nobility was seized and collectivised. In many cases the former owners were summarily executed and their private property was 'given to the people' (which is just a euphemism for 'given to the government') to create a land of equality and (so they said) prosperity for *all* the people, not just those greedy horrible private property owners...

In practice, when you abolish private ownership *everything* belongs to the government, *including the people*.

The Communist catch-cry, "From each according to his ability, to each according to his needs," quickly became, "From each, everything we can take; to each, as little as possible."

This was best encapsulated in a well-documented Soviet joke: *"We pretend to work, and they pretend to pay us."*

There was no incentive to be productive, because there was no reward. You could work as hard as you wanted, but you wouldn't benefit at all, so what was the incentive? The incentive was to get by doing as little as possible, and productivity quickly collapsed as a direct result.

But if, over the long term, we can only consume what we produce (or less), which is to say that our quality of life cannot exceed our production, then if productivity collapses, living standards must follow... and that's exactly what happened.

Again remember, it's not about how much money is changing hands, it's about the *other* side of every transaction—the goods or services being delivered in exchange for that money. Communism created a situation where people were given money even if they provided little or no value (work) in return.

Productivity tanked, living standards followed, and societal collapse was always going to be the ultimate destination.

People were promoted for party loyalty and for having connections, rather than for competence, creativity, or productivity, so people who had no business running a business were able to worm their way up within the Politburo and find themselves making decisions about prices, staffing, and supply for entire industries spanning the USSR from East Berlin in the West to Tajikistan in the South and to the farthest reaches of Siberia in the East, all from the comfort of a drab concrete office building in Moscow.

Mismanagement and misallocation of scarce resources was rife, productivity crashed further and famine was never far away. In fact starvation was weaponised by Joseph Stalin in the early 1930s, particularly against the people of Ukraine, in what they called the Holodomor, or 'death by hunger.'

Ukrainian peasant farmers had made the mistake of resisting this promised Communist utopia. They tried to stop the confiscation of their farms because they didn't want to be forced to farm on badly mismanaged state owned collectives when they already had their own land they could look after and pass on to their children, in accordance with God's design.

As punishment the Politburo imposed impossible production quotas, and when Ukraine's farmers failed to meet those quotas they were systematically raided and all possible foodstuffs were taken from them, including the grain they were going to use to plant next year's crop, ensuring millions would starve to death over a few years, peaking in 1933.

Those who left the region in search of food or work were captured or sent back by the police, who were the 'captains over a thousand and captains over fifty' which God warned about in 1 Samuel 8 and were loyal to the party. Those farmers who tried to steal some food (that they had grown on what used to be their own land!) for themselves or their families were executed.

The exact death toll is unknown, and the Soviet Union denied for decades that it ever happened, but with the fall of the Berlin wall in 1989 and the subsequent breaking up of the USSR and gradual release of various Soviet archives, there can no longer be any doubt that millions of Ukrainians died as a direct result of their government's policies, which were of course 'for the greater good' and done in pursuit of a Communist Utopia.

These were the policies which were going to bring about 'Heaven on Earth' as the government became god.

Then-US President Ronald Reagan once quipped that the nine most dangerous words in the English language are, *"I'm from the government and I'm here to help."* He made that joke at a time when the USSR was near the peak of its apparent powers and there were many within the USA who wanted to follow their example and attempt a Communist utopia of their own.

But his remark wasn't restricted only to utopian Communism, but also to the creeping welfare and regulatory state that was growing in the USA then and has multiplied since.

In Australia we have a reference point for just how much socialist thinking has overtaken our government thanks to a speech given by an influential Australian Prime Minister, Robert Menzies, on 10 November 1949:

"This is our great year of decision. Are we for the Socialist State, with its subordination of the individual to the universal officialdom of government, or are we for the ancient British faith that governments are the servants of the people, a faith

which has given fire and quality and direction to the whole of our history for six hundred years?...

"We must choose our road. Upon our decision will depend the future and fate of this nation. Every extension of Government power and control means less freedom of choice for the citizen. Government activities are monopolist. Monopolies exclude choice. No choice for the producer. No choice for the employee. No choice for the customer. The abolition of choice is the death of freedom. And in the end, what happens?

"Having chosen the Socialist Road, to what journey's end do we come? To the Master State, the one employer, the one planner, the one controller. In that State, as in the monstrous totalitarian States which have disfigured the history of the twentieth century, all free choice will have gone.

"The case against Socialism is a deadly one. It concerns the spiritual, mental, and physical future of our families.

"Socialism is not creative of real things. But by increasing enormously the circulation of money it creates an illusion of prosperity. By remaining indifferent to production it turns that illusion into a common fraud, money being worth less and less as there is more and more of it.

"The illusion of prosperity reduces the incentive to effort, and so production lags, and living standards actually fall. In Australia, our perils are for the time concealed by fancy prices paid to us by a hungry and ill-clad world.

"But in Great Britain, where there is in office a Socialist Government also, that government has been so busy creating the Socialist paradise of something for nothing that its own

supporters have difficulty in understanding why five years of Socialist rule have ended in a financial crisis, the devaluation of the currency, rising costs, and a new programme for further lowering the standard of living.

"The Socialist mouths such words as 'security,' by which he always means Government monetary payments. 'You need not build your own security,' he says; 'We, the Government, will provide it for you.'

"Let us analyse this piece of humbug. The best people in this community are not those who "leave it to the other fellow," but those who by thrift and self-sacrifice establish homes and bring up families and add to the national pool of savings and hope some day to sit under their own vine and fig tree, owing nothing to anybody."

It's an epic speech and rings powerfully today, even as we've failed to heed it in the seventy five years since.

The tragedy of that speech is that the party Robert Menzies founded, the Australian Liberal Party (our conservative party, similar to Republicans in the USA or Tories in the UK), is now *more socialist* than the Socialist Party that he was warning us against back in 1949.

Many years ago I gave a speech to a branch of the Victorian Liberal [Conservative] Party in which I simply read excerpts from Robert Menzies' full speech, and then asked, "If you were to look at the policies of the Modern Liberal Party would you think you were looking at the policies of the party Robert Menzies founded, or the party he was warning us against?"

I didn't need to answer my own rhetorical question because everyone already knew the answer, although it made many of them angry that they were faced with it so clearly.

The simple fact is that modern Western governments are what our ancestors would have called totalitarian monopolies, and if God characterised a 10% tax under a king as 'slavery,' as He did in 1 Samuel 8, what would He call what we have today?

The most charitable description for modern Western governments is 'benevolent tyrannies' which allow us the 'privilege' of choosing a new benevolent tyrant periodically.

If this seems over-blown or hyperbole to you then you've never tried to say 'no' to your government before.

Rosa Luxemburg, ironically a notable Marxist agitator in her day, rightly observed, *"I think those in motion have seen something the others have not; their imprisonment...* ***those who do not move, do not notice their chains."***

Rosa was a Marxist agitator and dedicated her life to the collectivist cause, but in this observation she was absolutely correct. I discovered this in the clearest possible way during Covid. It was those of us who 'tried to move' with freedom who discovered we were in chains. Those who cowered in their homes? They never saw the chains that held them.

If you do not try to move, to do something 'unauthorised,' then you will never notice the chains that keep you in place, and the danger is that you'll be completely enslaved in ways you don't even realise... until one day you decide to move.

If you don't believe your 'enlightened' Western government has you in chains, try refusing to fund one of their wars, taxpayer-funded abortions, or transgender surgery. Try saying something they don't approve of about a religion, sexuality, or some other 'protected' attribute. Try not taking a jab that they tell you to take... If you don't ever move from the spot they want you to be, you'll never notice your chains.

My few years in the military were the beginning of my shift from being a good little cookie-cutter-conservative to becoming a libertarian, because I was so confronted by the reality of the very flawed and very *human* organisation I'd so venerated throughout my upbringing, that it completely transformed my view of all government departments.

Then, thanks to over a decade of work as a political commentator starting in 2009, I was most certainly 'aware of my chains' before Covid madness took over my home city of Melbourne, Australia. Even so I was shocked at how quickly those chains went from being metaphorical to being literal in early 2020 as we were locked down under de facto martial law 'for our own good.'

The 'Covid-free' utopia promised by my government led to the closest thing to hell that Australia has experienced since it came into existence in 1901.

In order for mankind to fully prove that 'God is dead,' in order for government to fully step into the role of government-god that it so desperately craves, it must prove that it can create a utopia, a heaven made with human hands.

But just like the real Heaven, it's not for everybody. Not everyone is fit even for a man-made heaven, and so the question lingers... what to do with the unfit?

As mentioned, communist 'utopias' simply killed these 'unfit,' but other societies have tried other less extreme measures.

For example, Great Britain deported their criminals in the 1700s, mostly to Australia. They wanted to rid the British Isles of the 'criminal underclasses.' The idea was that if the British Isles could rid themselves of these undesirables then a perfect society would arise. This was the belief that underpinned the deportation of criminals to the far side of the world.

Other societies have simply sought to keep the 'undesirables' apart from their 'superior' counterparts. Apartheid South Africa is one such example, and the Segregation era in the United States is another. In this model the 'undesirables' are allowed to exist in a parallel society as long as they stay out of the way. Such practices are rightly condemned and have been ended, at least formally, decades ago.

But the human desire for perceived superiority over your fellow man, and the government's desire to create a utopia in defiance of God, remains.

Technology and times have changed, but people have not.

In Covid-panicked Australia, deportation of the unvaccinated undesirables wasn't possible, so instead the unjabbed were excluded from society in every way practicable.

It was a return of savagely enforced segregation, with no indignity or restriction considered 'too harsh.'

Many 'essential workers' were suddenly unable to work no matter how 'essential' they were deemed to be, and even when 'non-essential' workers were permitted to return to work many faced an immoral and unnecessary choice: take the jab against your conscience, and feed your family, or refuse the jab in compliance with your conscience, and step into an unknown future of unemployment and hungry kids.

This is clearly more civilised than killing the undesirables, and less extreme than deporting them, but this return of segregation should ring alarm bells and raise serious questions of how far we've come... or haven't come, as the case may be.

It's in moments like these that the Church becomes most important, for a healthy Church is the conscience of a culture.

But the Church was silent, or worse, the Church encouraged and supported the segregation and the suffering.

What happened?

A Closed Door

"Topher, I can't open the church. If I do, the government will take away the funding for the soccer academy!"

That's what my pastor said when I urged him in mid-2020 to reopen the church to in-person worship so we could fellowship on Sundays in person as well as support the poor and homeless and the increasing numbers of desperate people whose lives were being destroyed by Covid lockdowns.

"He can't even hear himself," I mulled ruefully.

There would have been no point quoting Matthew 6:24: *"No one can serve two masters, either you will hate the one and love the other, or you will cling to one and despise the other. You cannot serve God and money."*

The problem with my church and, quite frankly, *most* of the Church during Covid was far deeper than the theology of Matthew 6. It was idolatry, plain and simple.

My pastor wasn't going to open our church due to the government funding, but that was just the excuse. There was no way he was going to 'stick his neck out' and risk the wrath of the State whether it would have cost him money or not.

Let me be clear; I love the Church, and I loved that church in particular. I continued to support it even after they failed the moral test of Covid, and having now moved away from that area I have found a new church near my new home to fellowship with.

I'm not some out-of-fellowship lapsed Christian trying to point fingers at something I don't even support. I believe it is essential for Christians to be in fellowship with each other. The Church is the body of Christ and it's a beautiful and wonderful thing—I do not criticise it lightly!

But I will not be silent when the Church so obviously obeyed her fears and government rather than her faith and God, and in so doing failed the most serious test of faith in a generation.

What we saw from churches during Covid in Australia were closed doors, online-streamed services, and slavish adherence to mask mandates and segregation which separated worshippers on the basis of their 'vaccination' status.

But what *should* we have seen from churches? After all, there was a *pandemic!* The churches had to set an example of responsibility and loving care for others, right?

I have some idea of what the challenge of being a pastor looks like, having been raised as a pastor's son, with my oldest brother and a cousin also being pastors. I have seen clearly the challenges, expectations, demands, and sacrifices that good pastors make for their churches. I also understand that no matter what they do they will be criticised by *someone*, and for many pastors I'm just another chattering voice of ignorant criticism which they will studiously ignore.

I get it. And I'm not delusional enough to think that this book is going to bring many pastors to repentance no matter how much I think it should. Most will dismiss me as a worthless critic who doesn't 'get it.'

I also understand the overwhelming pressure on pastors to be respectable and responsible, to set a good example of a fine and upstanding citizen, to be a peacemaker, a 'force for good,' and in particular to look out for the welfare of the most vulnerable people in their congregation and their community.

And according to most pastors, that's what they did by their thousands around Australia and the world. They shut their doors, told people to obey the government health advice, repeated the mantra that 'staying home saves lives,' and supported the idea that a *temporary* ban on meeting together in person was really no harm at all to the Church and that church online was all that was needed to fulfil the biblical mandate to 'not forsake the gathering together of the saints.'

And after all was said and done, they told us from the pulpit that it was the *Christian* thing to do!

Whilst I don't expect many pastors to listen to me or care about my opinion, I still pray that such pastors will have a revelation from God and find it in themselves to repent of their idolatry, because limp acquiescence to a government claiming the status of god in our lives is exactly what the Church must *never* do.

"So then," you ask, "what *should* the Church do when there's a deadly pandemic about to ravage the land and kill untold thousands or millions of people?"

It's a great question with an astonishingly easy answer.

If death is coming, let's say the Black Death with a fatality rate over 30%... what do we do? We throw the doors open wide, move the sound system on to the steps, crank up the volume and cry out to any who will hear: "Repent, for your judgement day may be nearer than you think!"

If *death is coming,* forget hiding in fear because *lives* hang in the balance, instead be bold and courageous because *souls* hang in the balance!

The Church isn't a social club, charity, or soccer academy!

The Church holds the keys of salvation—nothing less than the eternal destiny of every human being—the Good News of the Gospel of Jesus Christ, the Way, the *only* Way to salvation!

Jesus is the *only* Way, Truth, and Life, so how can we *hide* just because death is coming? That's the opposite of our calling!

We worship the Creator of the universe and preach the Good News of God incarnate who has conquered sin and death and made a way for us to be reconciled to God the Father. As believers we are now seated with Him at the right hand of God the Father in heavenly places!!!

Do you believe that? Do you *really* believe that? Does your pastor believe that?

Of *course* your pastor believes that... right?

But actions speak louder than words.

Do their *actions* during Covid confirm that they believe they are the bearers of the soul-saving Good News, or that they are fearful of death just the same as nonbelievers?

How could anyone who truly believes in Jesus justify hiding their light under a bushel right at the very moment when it was most crucial for the world to hear the voice of truth?

Leave the saving of *lives* to others; the Church must get busy saving *souls*.

What the world needed to see and hear was courageous believers preaching the Good News. What they saw instead was fearful religious practitioners telling them to follow the government's instructions, get financial help from the government, and seek medical care from the government.

"Government-Ra'ah — Government is our guide."
"Government-Jireh — Government will provide."
"Government-Rapha — Government is our healer."

So said the Church, via a Zoom link whilst hiding safely behind firmly closed doors.

The Church's obedience to Covid restrictions was just a continuation of the idolatry which has been creeping into churches for decades.

Churches now are rarely just places of worship. Often they have associated childcare centres, charities for migrants or minorities, holiday programs for children, and as I discovered at my previous church, soccer academies.

These are not bad things! Charities are wonderful and we should be doing *more* of it. I'm not anti-charity! I have fond memories of church holiday programs during my own childhood, and I've personally worked with YWAM and numerous churches to support homeless men, drug addicts, and those with critical mental health issues... often in programs that receive government funding (not that I support the government funding, it's just that there's almost no program that doesn't!)

Soup kitchens are a great way to meet community needs and create opportunities to share the Good News, and childcare centres can be a great way for churches to outreach to their community whilst also bringing in revenue and reducing financial dependence on the Sunday offering, thanks to government support for those programs...

All of that is great, right? It's a win-win... isn't it? Outreach and revenue all rolled into one neat package!

But the question that needs to be asked is *why* a given church has chosen those specific activities. Was it the leading of God? Was it because God in his providence brought in a new member of the congregation with a set of skills and experience that opened up the opportunity? Was it because the community was so obviously in desperate need?

Well yes, sometimes. But most of the time? It's because they could get funding for that particular activity.

Funding from whom?

The government. Government-Jireh—Government will provide.

And I get it! At first it seems wonderful! There are new opportunities to connect with the community, there's added revenue in the door which allows an expansion in other programs or perhaps an increase in the pastoral staff, and to cap it all off now the Church is building relationships with local, state, or even federal government, with the perks and sense of importance that this brings!

But there's a dark side that creeps in, unseen at first.

You cannot serve two masters. Either you will hate one and love the other, or you will *despise* one and *cling to* the other.

I believe it is the latter which the Church did during Covid.

These churches expanded with their budgets inflated by government grants, believing this new government revenue was a *gift from God* because it allowed them to increase the paid hours of pastoral staff and maybe do some extra things in Sunday School or provide a little bus for the elderly or disabled, or any one of a million other things. That's *great*, but once that money is budgeted for it becomes *needed* and the threat of losing it is a serious threat indeed.

With money comes compromise. It may seem small at first—the pastor simply choosing not to address certain topics in a Sunday sermon to ensure he's being 'inclusive,' because being inclusive is one of the prerequisites to being a 'partner' in some government-funded program or other, or perhaps buying in to the idea that 'politics doesn't belong in the pulpit,' because that's easier than risking biting the political hand that feeds you.

Small step by small step churches become neutered, pastors fall silent on the very issues where their voices are most needed, and what was once a place where God was worshipped without fear becomes a place where the latest government agenda item takes priority for budget reasons.

So when Covid comes along and the government tells churches to shut their doors temporarily, the unspoken threat is clear. If the funding is pulled then these churches will be closing their doors permanently because the government money they now depend on will be gone for good, so they 'go along to get along,' becoming 'responsible and upstanding citizens' and setting an example of compliance with government because 'it's the Christian thing to do'—and besides, Romans 13 said so...

They dress it up in religious language to make it sound virtuous, but for many churches the doors were not closed to keep Covid out, but *to keep the money flowing in*.

The closed doors sent a clear message to those desperate and hurting people who were locked out of their work and businesses, shunned by friends and family, neglected by professional counsellors, and demonised by media and politicians for simply wanting to survive and to provide for themselves and their families in exactly the way God commanded them to do. Those people came looking for answers, looking for hope, and some of them even came looking for God. They found a closed door which said:

"The answers you seek are not here."

"We're as afraid as you are."

"Our God hasn't provided for us either."

"The God we serve isn't available to you when you need him most."

Or;

"All God's operators are busy right now, but your call is important to us, please try again another time when we're not scared to death."

I know that desperate people were being turned away by the Church in droves, because many of them reached out to me when they ran out of all other options. More than a few of them went on to take their own lives.

Not to put too fine a point on it, but for those pastors who obeyed the government fully and without question, I do sincerely wonder what they believe the Church exists to do.

If a pandemic is *not* the time for the Church to fill its pews with seekers… then when is?

They shut their doors and told people to go and beg the government for help, "Oh, but be sure to tune in to the livestream on Sunday, and don't forget to tithe.'

If you are more concerned with lives than with souls then you don't understand why Jesus died and rose again or why God made the Church to preach the Good News.

It was not always like this. Once upon a time missionaries went specifically to where the people were dying, places such as leper colonies, at great personal risk and with no prospect of financial or other rewards, specifically to preach the gospel and provide medical care to the 'outcasts,' because they cared about saving souls even if it cost them their own life.

Today the Church joins the pile-on to ostracise the outcasts and berate them for not doing 'the Christian thing,' by which they mean meekly staying locked in their homes and rolling up their sleeves for an experimental jab because 'it's what Jesus would have done.'

God takes His name very seriously and we've seen already how government has usurped many of the names of God in its effort to become a god of its own making.

But what the Church did during Covid wasn't just idolatry, it was blasphemy.

The Church took the name of God in vain.

The third commandment is that we should not 'take the name of the Lord your God in vain.' It was third in the list, right after not making idols, and *before* not committing murder.

God takes His name seriously—as seriously as murder. In ancient times, a false prophet could be stoned once their words did not come true. Why? Because a prophet would claim to be speaking *in the name of God*. A prophet was considered a prophet because it was believed that God had spoken to him, and when he spoke, he spoke in God's name.

"Thus saith the Lord..."

If that person was found to be a liar, or even just wrong, then they had to be stoned. They were a false prophet—they had taken the name of the Lord in vain and committed blasphemy, and this was punishable by death.

Today we don't use the phrase 'Thus saith the Lord' because we've replaced it with a more modern, and much more manipulative alternative:

"The Christian thing to do is..."

That's the modern version of 'Thus saith the Lord.'

"The Christian thing to do is to get the jab."

Is it? Is that the Bible speaking, or your fear?

"It's what Jesus would do because it's safe and effective."

What if you're wrong?

What if you're saying the 'Christian thing' is to accept a 'vaccine' that turns out to neither be safe, nor very effective, and isn't even a vaccine but rather an experimental gene therapy that causes many immediate adverse reactions, including fatal ones, and is now ravaging people in unexpected ways including with neurological issues and turbo cancers?

And you told people to take it in the name of the Lord Jesus Christ???

Pastors lined up on Sundays in their thousands to urge their congregations to obey the government, accept historically unprecedented restrictions on their God-given freedoms including their freedom to assemble with the saints, and ultimately to go and participate in the world's largest and riskiest clinical trial because it was the *Christian* thing to do.

They took the name of the Lord in vain.

And they simultaneously committed idolatry by accepting the government's claim that the government has the authority to tell Christians how and when to worship.

The example of Daniel in the Bible is our best example of what the Church ought to have done instead.

When King Darius made a law that he and *only* he could be worshipped and prayed to as god, Daniel was put in a tough spot. Daniel was a God-fearing man who had a great relationship with King Darius personally, and unknown to Darius, Daniel was actually the *target* of this new law. Other influential administrators felt threatened by the foreign, God-fearing Daniel and had hatched a plot to get rid of him.

Daniel prayed three times every day, facing out an open window towards Jerusalem. It was a very public act of faith for a man in captivity in a foreign land, and the administrators used it as their trap.

After the law was passed, making any prayers to anyone other than Darius punishable by death, Daniel continued to pray "just as he had done before" [Daniel 6:10], and it's this detail which ought to have guided the Church's response to Covid restrictions on worship.

"Just as he had done before."

In other words, in response to the decree from the king, *nothing* changed.

Daniel *could* have simply closed the windows and prayed while hidden, or prayed at a different time of day, after dark with the lights off, or hidden his worship to God in any one of dozens of ways.

Why didn't he?

Because his obedience to God in *defiance* of the king was the point. Doing it "just as he had done before" *was the point.*

If Daniel had changed his worship *at all* in response to the king then he would be placing the king's words above his allegiance to God. He did everything "just as he had done before" in order to make it clear that he obeyed God first, and God *only.*

It's interesting to note that there's no clear instruction from God that Daniel had to pray to Him three times per day. That's not found in the law of Moses, and the modern Jewish custom of praying three times per day is found in the Talmud, written long after Daniel was dead.

In the Talmud the prayer three times per day is based on the prayers of Abraham (morning), Isaac (afternoon) and Jacob (evening), so there is a connection to pre-Daniel history, but it's a custom that emerged long after Daniel and there is no clear biblical injunction requiring Daniel to do this, nor had the custom yet appeared in Jewish culture.

So this begs the question, why couldn't Daniel just change how he worshipped? It wouldn't have been a sin to pray in secret or to pray only once at night!

It wouldn't really be a compromise... it wouldn't really be breaking the word of God... and it would have spared him his life and protected the *position of influence which God had given him*, so surely this is one of those times where you just go along to get along, right?

Why cause trouble? Just be a respectable and upstanding member of the community—you're in Darius' trusted circle, life is good, and think of all the *good you can do* if you just go along to get along. You're not *really* compromising on God's word at all...

... and besides, maybe God *put* you in this position, walking the halls of power, so you can *do good* at some crucial time in the future... maybe being too stubborn now will cause you to miss your chance to *really* make a difference later...

All this and more would have been whispered by Satan into Daniel's ear the day he heard about the decree by Darius, just as it was whispered into the ears of pastors worldwide as lockdowns and restrictions took hold.

But what would it have said about Daniel, his faith, and his God, if Daniel changed how he worshipped in order to *appear* to comply with the order from Darius?

What would have been the message to Darius? To the other Jewish captives? And to God himself?

It would have said that Daniel was an idolater. That he was afraid. That his trust was in Darius and the wealth and power that came from being in Darius' trusted circle, and that this position of privilege was more valuable to Daniel than to be seen to be a faithful servant of God.

It would have said about Daniel exactly what it *did* say about modern churches when they closed their doors and told everyone to worship online because the government said so.

Daniel's continued prayer, in defiance of Darius, was not about his obedience to God in the strict sense—to stop praying at the open window three times a day would not have been a sin in itself—but it was about the status of God in Daniel's life and whether he was putting God first and making it known that God was number one.

Daniel was willing to die just to avoid creating the *appearance* that he feared Darius more than he feared God, even though in *practice* he could have spent just as much time in prayer in the privacy of his bedroom behind a closed window!

It was about what that closed window would have *said* to the world outside about Daniel's God, just like Covid was about what the closed doors of the Church *said* to the hurting and desperate world.

This is a hard word, and I know from experience talking with pastors and speaking at church conferences that many pastors are unwilling to hear it and are offended by it!

'How dare you' or 'you don't understand' are the kinds of responses I've learned to expect.

But some pastors are willing to listen. I've had the privilege of speaking with a small but growing number of pastors whose eyes have been opened and they have repented and committed themselves to *never* compromise like that again. They are committed to following the example of Daniel next time, although we all hope there won't be a 'next time'!

God is a God of second chances, and God knows I've needed second, fifth, and tenth chances throughout my life! I want to make it clear that I do not stand in judgement or condemnation of pastors and church elders who compromised during Covid, but nor will I be silent in the face of what I sincerely believe to be a widespread moral failure of the Church in the face of the greatest moral test of our generation.

It is when the world is most gripped by fear that we must go forward with the greatest faith. It is when mortal lives are in peril that we must risk the most to save eternal souls. It is when the government seeks to control our worship that we must stand most firmly and without compromise.

To alter our worship to God on the say-so of government is to place government over God and commit idolatry. I've no doubt that Covid is not the last time in my lifetime that the Church will be tested in this way. I hope and pray that more pastors and church leaders recognise their error, repent, and commit themselves to never repeating these mistakes.

Let us never again put the keys to eternal life behind a closed door in the moment of the world's greatest need.

What About Romans 13?

Ah yes, probably the most-asked question I get when I speak on this subject:

"What about Romans 13?"

I'll address this head on, and include in this chapter a discussion on 1 Peter 2:13 for good measure.

Let's start by reading the key passage in full:

Let every soul be subject to the governing authorities. For there is no authority except from God, and the authorities that exist are appointed by God. Therefore whoever resists the authority resists the ordinance of God, and those who resist will bring judgement on themselves. For rulers are not a terror to good works, but to evil. Do you want to be unafraid of the authority? Do what is good, and you will have praise from the same. For he is God's minister to you for good. But if you do evil, be afraid; for he does not bear the sword in vain; for he is God's minister, an avenger to execute wrath on him who practices evil. Therefore you must be subject, not only because of wrath but also for conscience' sake. For because of this you also pay taxes, for they are God's ministers attending continually to this very thing. Render therefore to all their due: taxes to whom taxes are due, customs to whom customs, fear to whom fear, honour to whom honour.

— Romans 13:1-7

At face value that seems pretty clear cut! We as Christians must clearly and unequivocally do as we're told by *every* civil authority and government!

Except that's not what anyone believes. Not even Paul who wrote that passage!

There's not a single Christian on the planet that believes that passage should be taken in full, as absolute, in isolation, without also consulting the rest of Scripture on this topic, and I can prove it.

At various moments in history and in various places on earth, governments and civil authorities have written laws requiring participation in murder. Yes, OK, I'll happily fall foul of Godwin's law and mention the Nazis as exhibit A.

Does any Christians seriously think that the Nazi Party's laws and orders to report any Jews found hiding so they could be rounded up and exterminated was an order to which Christians were required to be subject?

If any do, I haven't met them yet. The Nazis practised conscription, ordering people to guard and operate extermination camps where humans were murdered en-mass, and it was all *legal* according to German law and courts. Should Christians who were conscripted and ordered to murder Jews, Gypsies, and disabled people have obeyed because Romans 13 said so?

This was a real question for German Christians, and it proves the point: we *know* that Romans 13 isn't the whole story!

"Yes, of course," many object, "but we should only disobey civil authorities if they're ordering us to disobey God directly."

OK, I agree, but that's not what that passage says. Romans 13 makes no caveats, no ifs, buts, maybes, whys, or wherefores.

It says, "Do as you're told. End of story."

So how do you know that there's a caveat about when the civil authorities are ordering you to break God's law? Because you know that you must take into account the whole counsel of Scripture, that's how.

It's the whole counsel of Scripture that teaches us that God's law is higher than man's law, and that when we're forced to choose which one we will obey we, have an obligation to obey God and disobey man.

That's not from Romans 13 explicitly (although actually it kind of is, we'll get to that later), but every Christian believes it. So my first point on Romans 13 is that it's not some special stand-alone scripture which captures every nuance of the issue of obedience to civil government. It must be taken in context with the rest of Scripture.

The same is true in 1 Peter:

Therefore submit yourselves to every ordinance of man for the Lord's sake, whether to the king as supreme, or to governors, as to those who are sent by him for the punishment of evildoers and for the praise of those who do good. For this is the will of God, that by doing good you may put to silence the ignorance of foolish men—as free, yet not using liberty as a cloak for vice, but as bondservants of God. Honour all people. Love the brotherhood. Fear God. Honour the king.

— 1 Peter 2:13-17

Submit yourselves to *every ordinance of man*? I don't know a single Christian who truly believes that's what we as Christians are required by God to do all the time in every place. Every

Christian I've ever spoken with acknowledges that at certain times in history and in certain places on earth it has been morally *required* of Christians to disobey civil authorities.

And that makes sense when you consider that even Paul and Peter, the authors of those passages, didn't believe in absolute obedience to civil authorities.

Paul met Jesus on his way to Damascus, he was blinded for three days, had his eyes opened by Ananias and then started preaching in the synagogue that Jesus is the Son of God.

When the synagogue leaders in Damascus planned to kill him did he say, "Oh well, they're a civil authority and I have to be subject to them?"

No, his followers let him down over the wall of the city and he ran away, directly defying the wishes of the leaders of that city and carrying on preaching his 'heresy' about Jesus.

Peter did the same after Herod imprisoned him and he was miraculously released by an angel in Acts 25. Not only did he gladly depart from the prison, in direct violation of the civil authority of King Herod, but he went off and continued doing the very things he had been imprisoned for!

And this behaviour is by no means unusual. Scripture is *full* of examples of righteous people disobeying civil authorities.

The wise men directly disobeyed Herod's order that they return to him and tell him where they found the baby "king of the Jews" [Matthew 2].

The Jewish midwives lied to Pharaoh when they claimed that Jewish women were 'vigorous' in giving birth, meaning the midwives arrived too late to kill the newborn sons as Pharaoh had commanded them [Exodus 1].

We've already discussed Daniel and his choice not only to continue to pray to God, but to pray *publicly* just as he had done before.

Then there's David before he became king. He was on the run and in a moment of desperate hunger he and his men ate the ceremonial bread meant only for the priests. The penalty for David eating it should have been death [1 Samuel 21].

A thousand years later Jesus pointed to David's act of disobedience to *God's* law when His disciples were accused by the Pharisees of breaking the Sabbath because they plucked and ate corn on the holy Sabbath day:

"Have you not read what David did when he was hungry, he and those who were with him: how he entered the house of God and ate the showbread which was not lawful for him to eat, nor for those who were with him, but only for the priests? Or have you not read in the law that on the Sabbath the priests in the temple profane the Sabbath, and are blameless? Yet I say to you that in this place there is One greater than the temple. But if you had known what this means, 'I desire mercy and not sacrifice,' you would not have condemned the guiltless. For the Son of Man is Lord even of the Sabbath."

— Matthew 12:3-8

Jesus makes it abundantly clear that David was not considered evil for having violated *God's* laws in that particular instance. And Jesus Himself uses David's actions as a precedent to explain the disciples' actions one thousand years later.

Jesus also gives us a clue as to *why* these people were justified in their actions even though they violated the law of Moses.

In verse 7 He says, *"But if you had known what this means, 'I desire mercy and not sacrifice,' you would not have condemned the guiltless."*

Jesus is declaring David guiltless, as well as His disciples, on the basis that God desires *mercy* and not *sacrifice*.

What's that about? Mercy and not sacrifice? And somehow that makes eating the showbread and picking corn on the Sabbath OK?

What this is pointing to is what Paul talked about in Romans 2, the 'circumcision of the heart.' In that passage Paul explicitly rejected the idea that a physical circumcision was still a requirement to follow God, an idea that Jewish believers were struggling with. Paul argued forcefully that outward obedience alone was useless and that God was concerned with the obedience of the heart.

Jesus' reference to David in Matthew 12 is clear evidence that this was *always* true—even in Old Testament times God desired compassion rather than sacrifice, a circumcision of the *heart* rather than the body.

This is essentially an instruction to 'use your head.' It shows that whilst obedience to the law (including to civil authorities) should be our *default* position, we are allowed to weigh up a circumstance and come to the conclusion that slavish obedience to the law is the wrong thing in a specific case.

This is why God gives each of us a conscience of our own. A conscience would be completely redundant and silly if all we were supposed to do was slavishly obey a set of rules without ever having to weigh the moral implications for ourselves.

God gave you a conscience; He expects you to use it.

Let me finish these biblical examples with the great Queen Esther, one of the most badass women of the Bible. Having been hand-picked as the most beautiful woman in the most powerful kingdom of her time and been made the queen, Esther was then informed of a plot to kill her Jewish kin. She knew she had been placed into her position *by God* so she could save her people, but even *God's* plan was going to require her to break the law!

Esther 4 covers this moment in the story when she resolves to go and speak to her husband the king and see if she can save her people, but the catch is that even though she was the queen she didn't have the rights that women today enjoy. It was against the law for her to approach the king, her husband, unless he called for her, and if she approached him and the king didn't want to see her then she could be put to death.

That was the law of the land, the law that a strict reading of Romans 13 or 1 Peter 2 would say she had to *obey.* But what did she actually do?

In Esther 4:16 she says to her supporters, *"Go, gather together all the Jews who are present in Shushan, and fast ye for me; and neither eat nor drink three days, night or day. I also and my maidens will fast likewise. And so will I go in unto the king, which is not according to the law; and if I perish, I perish."*

This is pre-meditated lawbreaking by Queen Esther.

The Bible is *full* of heroes of the faith *breaking the law* for a good cause! Sometime to relieve the suffering of others or to save lives (Esther and the Jewish midwives), sometimes to preach the gospel (Paul and Peter), sometimes to set an example of obedience to God against the wishes of the king (Daniel), and sometimes because they were desperately hungry and in dire straights (David and his men).

The idea that the laws of men or even the laws of *God* are completely and absolutely 100% ironclad and never to be breached under any circumstances simply isn't biblical.

Yes, I said what I said.

Now let me quickly add a caveat which I'll be diving into in detail later on, but it would be remiss of me not to mention now: You are responsible before God for your actions and any time you choose to disobey God's laws, and anytime you choose to disobey man's laws, you'd better be certain that your heart is right before God and that you're doing it absolutely 100% for the right reasons (more on the 'right reasons' shortly), because if you're not... well, it really doesn't bear thinking about.

I'm very mindful of the verses in Matthew 18 where Jesus says it would be better for me to have a millstone hung around my neck and be drowned in the depths of the sea than to lead one of His 'little ones' astray, and you'd better believe I'm mindful of the fact that concepts such as 'Christian civil disobedience' are ripe for abuse and misuse by those of bad faith and selfish intent.

But my conscience will not allow me to stay silent, so as I write I pray for God to guide my every word and to guide every reader to understand what it is that I am, and am *not*, saying.

In the famous words of Martin Luther, "To go against conscience is neither right nor safe. Here I stand, I can do no other, so help me God. Amen."

He may well have thought those would be his final publicly recorded words, because he was facing his inquisitors and would reasonably have expected execution to swiftly follow his defiance. God had other ideas, but final words or not Luther's declaration rings true when considered against the backdrop of the whole counsel of Scripture.

But beware, because just as Paul warns us in Romans not to use God's grace as an excuse to sin, so also we must not use the principles of obedience to conscience before God as an excuse to be selfish, wilful, prideful, or presumptuous. More on that later.

For now it is enough to say that the Bible is absolutely clear: God allows us to disobey and even defy civil authorities under the right circumstances and for the right reasons.

Consider Psalm 94:20-21:

Shall the throne of iniquity, which devises evil by law,
Have fellowship with You?
They gather together against the life of the righteous,
And condemn innocent blood.

Notice the phrase "evil by law." This passage is speaking of a legitimate king on a real throne writing real laws in a real kingdom, and asking rhetorically whether you can really have fellowship with a throne that devises evil by law.

That's the New King James Version. The New Century Version renders it this way:

"Crooked leaders cannot be your friends. They use the law to cause suffering."

Psalm 94:20 makes it crystal clear that just because something is the law doesn't make it right. This passage speaks of "evil by law" and kings who "use the law to *cause* suffering." It's clear that there's a higher principle here than simply 'it's the law.'

The law itself is subject to a higher law, God's law, and man's laws which do evil, cause suffering, or permit injustice, are no laws at all, so says Psalm 94.

And it is our conscience that alerts us to when one law breaks the other.

Psalm 94 seems to contradict Romans 13 and 1 Peter 2, but we know that all of the Bible is God's word all of the time, so there has to be a way to reconcile these scriptures so that we can obey Romans 13 *and* Psalm 94 at the same time, and indeed there is.

But before we get to that, we need to lay the foundation of using one scripture to correct the interpretation of another, which is what I'm doing with Psalm 94 vs Romans 13.

Let's consider the example of Jesus when He was tempted in the wilderness in Matthew 4. Satan tried to deceive Jesus using Scripture:

Then the devil took Him [Jesus] *to the holy city and had Him stand on the highest point of the temple. "If You are the Son of God," he said, "throw Yourself down. For it is written:*

"'He will command His angels concerning you, and they will lift you up in their hands, so that you will not strike your foot against a stone.'"

— Matthew 4:5-6

Satan is correct that the Scriptures say this, but that's not *all* they say on the subject. Jesus immediately replies in verse 7: ***"It is also written**: 'Do not put the Lord your God to the test.'"*

Jesus is not saying the verse about angels lifting him up is wrong, He's saying it's not the whole story.

This shows us *from Scripture* that we cannot derive our entire theology on any topic from just *one scripture.* The whole counsel of Scripture must be considered, and you can answer scripture with scripture, using verses from throughout the Bible to correct and guide the understanding of others.

With that in mind let's go back to Romans 13 and read it again, to see if perhaps *within* these seven verses we'll find the understanding that allows us to reconcile these verses with Psalm 94.

Let's re-read Romans 13:1-7, with new emphasis added:

Let every soul be subject to the governing authorities. For there is no authority except from God, and the authorities that exist are appointed by God Therefore whoever resists the authority resists the ordinance of God, and those who resist will bring judgement on themselves. For ***rulers are not a terror to good***

works, but to evil*. Do you want to be unafraid of the authority? Do what is good, and you will have praise from the same. For he is* ***God's minister to you for good****. But if you do evil, be afraid; for he does not bear the sword in vain; for he is* ***God's minister, an avenger to execute wrath on him who practices evil****. Therefore you must be subject, not only because of wrath but* ***also for conscience' sake****.*

Notice that built into these verses is the *purpose* of government, which is to reward good and punish evil.

That is no mere detail. Paul says the authorities which exist are appointed by God *for the purpose* of punishing evil and rewarding good.

But what do we do when the government is not fulfilling its God-given purpose? When the government is executing wrath *not* on those who do evil, but those who do good?

Paul was familiar with this problem. He was hounded by evil civil authorities for decades, and in his earlier life, as a synagogue 'authority,' he *himself* committed acts of unspeakable evil against Christians including murder.

And then after his conversion Paul was a man who chose *not* to obey civil authorities throughout his ministry.

So how can he tell us to obey when he didn't do it himself? How can he say God has instituted government to punish evil when even *he* experienced them punishing good?

Because he's *not* telling us to obey all the time no matter what, he's telling us to obey by default when those authorities are fulfilling their God-given purpose of punishing evil and rewarding good.

The *purpose* for which God has instituted these authorities is *built in* to the instruction to obey them for a reason. It's a condition. When these authorities betray that purpose they no longer act with the authority they've been given by God, and we are no longer required by God to obey them, in fact quite the opposite.

But there's more.

Paul tells us to obey for *conscience' sake*, which is to say, "Obey so that you can have a clear conscience."

That's all well and good when the laws of the civil authorities are in harmony with the laws of God and can therefore be obeyed with a clear conscience . In such a moment we are absolutely morally obligated to obey!

But what if government betrays its God-given purpose and writes laws that are evil, permit injustice, or cause suffering, as in Psalm 94? What if it's not possible to have a clear conscience before God *and* man? What if the laws written by men force you to choose between obeying God or man?

Man made idolatrous governments will start to reward evil, punish good, call evil good and good evil, do injustice, and permit evil by law.

Man made governments will begin to *replace* God, and it's only a matter of time before they write laws that are not compatible with a clear conscience before God.

When that happens you can *either* have a clear conscience before God, *or* a clear conscience before men, but not both.

In that context Paul's admonition to obey the civil authorities *for conscience' sake* takes on an entirely new dimension. I hope you will agree that we must have a clear conscience before God, first and foremost, and that *if* it is not possible to have a clear conscience before God *and* man then it's because man has written laws which defy God in some way, laws which permit injustice, cause suffering, and do evil rather than good.

If it isn't possible to have a clear conscience before God and man it's because man is trying to *become* god. Mankind is redefining good and evil, legalising injustice, and causing suffering by statute.

God made civil authorities for the purpose of rewarding good and punishing evil. Satan takes hold of them and twists them to steal, to kill, and to destroy.

1 Peter 2 is even more explicit on this point. Let's re-read the key passage of verses 13-17 with new emphasis added:

Therefore submit yourselves to every ordinance of man ***for the Lord's sake****, whether to the king as supreme, or to governors, as to those who are sent by him* ***for the punishment of evildoers and for the praise of those who do good****. For this is the will of God,* ***that by doing good you may put to silence the ignorance of foolish men****—as free, yet* ***not using liberty as a cloak for vice****, but as bondservants of God. Honour all people. Love the brotherhood. Fear God. Honour the king.*

See how this passage already contains all of the caveats which I've laid out above? This passage clearly states that our obedience is for the Lord's sake, which means it's *never* going to be in defiance of our conscience before God.

Our conscience is central to this whole issue so it's important to distinguish between our conscience and our will. Scripture is full of instructions to do things we don't *want* to do, things that may be against our *will* or our selfish flesh which we are instructed to crucify daily.

But if we are walking with Christ and are a new creation with a new and circumcised heart then at no point are we instructed by Scripture to do anything that is against our *conscience*.

Paul is quite clear on this when he's instructing believers to *not* use their liberty to offend the conscience of weaker believers:

But be careful that your freedom does not cause those who are weak in faith to fall into sin. Suppose one of you who has knowledge [here, Paul is talking about knowledge that it is *not* sinful to eat meat sacrificed to idols] *eats in an idol's temple. Someone who is weak in faith might see you eating there and be encouraged to eat meat sacrificed to idols while* ***thinking it is wrong to do so****. This weak believer for whom Christ died is ruined because of your 'knowledge.' When you sin against your brothers and sisters in Christ like this and cause them to do what they feel is wrong, you are also sinning against Christ.*

— 1 Corinthians 8:9-13

Two points from this scripture: first, we must be *very careful* about practising Christian civil disobedience and be *really certain* that it is a matter of our own conscience before God, because if it's anything less than a matter of conscience before God (for example if we're disobeying man's laws just as a matter of 'freedom' or convenience or money but not for our own conscience' sake) and our disobedience becomes a stumbling block to another 'weaker' believer, then we've sinned against Christ.

This is serious stuff and this alone should cause you to take this topic *very* seriously and really search your soul and make sure your heart is right before God before you engage in civil disobedience!

Second, each believer is bound to act in accordance with their own conscience, even when their theology is wrong. Now, don't misunderstand me. I'm not suggesting that 'everyone is right' and I'm certainly not suggesting that there's any way to God other than through Christ, but it's clear in this scripture that we *must* act in accordance with our own conscience and what we *believe* to be right, and trust that God will guide us and teach us where our beliefs are wrong.

In the example Paul gives, the believer whose conscience has no problem with eating meat sacrificed to idols can do so and it is *not* sin, while for the believer who believes it *is* sin... it becomes sin!

The difference is not the act, the act of putting the meat in your mouth, chewing, and swallowing, isn't the sin, it's the impact on the *conscience* of the one committing the act that makes it either sin, or not, according to their conscience.

So when Paul instructs us to obey the civil authorities "for conscience's sake" it's no mere aside. Your conscience is crucial to this whole issue and we *must act in accordance with our conscience before God.*

Even more, out of respect for the conscience of weaker believers, we must be careful that we *only* practice Christian civil disobedience in areas where our own conscience would be seared if we did not. To practice Christian civil disobedience flippantly is to risk harming the faith of a weaker believer.

We must always have concern for the impact that our actions may have on weaker believers and I believe that means we must only practice Christian civil disobedience to the degree that *our own conscience* requires. In the words of Martin Luther, "Here I stand, *I can do no other.*" I believe the concept of 'I can do no other' is really important here... it is acceptable to engage in Christian civil disobedience only when to *not* disobey would compromise your own conscience. Only when you 'can do no other.'

You get the idea. Let's get back to the purpose of government.

God created government "for the punishment of evildoers and for the praise of those who do good," and notice in 1 Peter 2:15 the purpose statement, that *"**by doing good** you may put to silence the ignorance of foolish men."*

This is the *purpose* for which we are called to obey—to put to silence the ignorance of fooling men by *doing good.*

Not "by obeying," not "by doing what you're told," not "by following orders." That is not the pathway by which we are instructed to "put to silence the ignorance of foolish men," no, it is by "doing good."

So the purpose of Peter's instruction to obey is that we *do good.* In that context can this verse really be construed as an instruction to do *evil* just because the civil authorities said so? Of course not!

The whole purpose of our obedience to civil authorities is so that we will *do good, for the Lord's sake,* to keep a *clear conscience before God,* and *put to silence foolish men.*

Once you see it you can't unsee it. The caveats and 'conditions' placed on our obedience to civil authorities are right there in these scriptures, and now it all makes sense alongside Psalm 94:20:

"Crooked leaders cannot be your friends, they use the law to cause suffering."

Neither Paul nor Peter said we should just 'do as we're told' by the government. It's us who mistranslated it.

Many readers will rightly be wondering why Paul and Peter used such 'absolute' language, words like 'submit' and 'be subject,' if they never meant it to be completely absolute. If it was less about obedience and more about doing good in accordance with your conscience, then why did they say 'obey' in the first place? That's a great question.

To answer it we must go back to the original Greek and observe that Peter and Paul both chose *not* to use the most absolute version of the Greek word for 'obey.'

The strongest form of 'obey' in ancient Greek is *'hupakouo,'* according to Thayer's Greek Lexicon, and from the time of Herodotus onward this word *hupakouo* was used to say 'obey absolutely.' That means that for over four hundred years prior to the birth of Christ, *hupakouo* was the strongest and most absolute form of the word 'obey' in the Greek language.

This is *not* the word used in either Romans 13 or 1 Peter 2. In both passages the word used is the softer form, 'Hupatasso.' It still broadly means to 'obey,' but without the same 'absolute' sense to it.

This was not an accident.

We know for a fact that both Paul and Peter were aware of this more absolute form of the word 'obey,' because Paul uses it many times elsewhere in Romans as well as in numerous epistles to the various Churches, and Peter uses it in 1 Peter 3, the very next chapter after he chose *not* to use it in relation to obeying civil authorities.

So Paul's choice not to use this absolute form of 'obey' in Romans 13, and Peter's choice not to use it in 1 Peter 2, was a *choice.* They *could* have used the most absolute form of the word available, and they chose to use a softer form of the word 'obey' instead.

Why? Because they were not saying to obey absolutely, and they never meant for these verses to be translated or understood that way. That was *our* mistake in the translation and teaching of these passages, not their mistake in the original Greek.

So for the avoidance of doubt let me close out this chapter with what I believe to be our responsibilities as Christians when it comes to civil authority, based on the whole counsel of Scripture *including* but not limited to Romans 13, 1 Peter 2, and Psalm 94:

- As Christians we are to be peaceful, orderly, and obedient by default, to set a good example, and to preserve the good reputation of the name of Christ.

- We are to recognise that civil authority is instituted by God for the noble purpose of rewarding good and punishing evil, and as far as our conscience will allow, it should be respected as a God-appointed minister.

- Christian civil disobedience must be a matter of conscience for us, not just a matter of convenience or will, and must be in areas where government has overstepped its God-given authority and created laws which cannot be obeyed with a clear conscience before God.

- We must be very careful not to offend the conscience of a weaker brother by exercising our own freedom for freedom's sake. This highlights the need for disobedience to be a matter of our own conscience and nothing less.

- When we do engage in Christian civil disobedience we must do so only to the extent required by our conscience, and continue to respect lawful authority in all areas where our conscience will allow it.

- We must always be careful that our disobedience is for the purpose of *doing good* and that we do all things for the *Lord's sake*.

You may rightly ask how civil disobedience could possibly be 'for the Lord's sake,' and that's another great question, which I will answer next.

Disobedience for Christ's Sake

No, I'm not swearing in this chapter title, I promise!

In this chapter we're literally going to talk about what disobedience "for the sake of the Lord Jesus Christ" would look like.

Thankfully we don't have to look far, because lots of people in history have set examples for us.

Ask yourself what was better for the Lord's sake: that some churches in Germany during the rise of the Nazi party and during World War II displayed Nazi flags and supported the duly elected leader Adolf Hitler in accordance with their nation's laws? Or that some churches and Christians passionately spoke out against Hitler, refused to comply, and were imprisoned or even executed for their disobedience?

Yes, that was a very particular moment in history, but it would be naïve to think that we won't see a repeat of such horrors in the Western world in the decades and centuries to come. In fact, I'd say it's inevitable given that Satan will stop at nothing to destroy humanity, and humans haven't changed.

If our theology is going to work at all it has to work in moments and places like Nazi Germany, because it is moments and places like that in which we will *most* rely on God and need His wisdom and guidance for our lives, and it's in moments like that where it is most important for us to make the right moral choices.

So which is better? The ones who 'obeyed every civil authority' in Germany in accordance with the strict (and incorrect) preaching of Romans 13, or the ones who practised Psalm 94 and refused to be allied to that 'throne'?

Which did more to protect and glorify the name and reputation of Christ? Which can truly say they had a clean conscience before God?

The history of the Church during Nazi-era Germany is complex, with *many* heroes, many anti-heroes, and many outright villains. Some great books have been written on the subject, so I will merely touch briefly on two great characters.

Martin Niemoller was a man on the right side of history, and more importantly on the right side of his conscience. He is best known today for his famous quote:

"First they came for the socialists, and I did not speak out because I was not a socialist. Then they came for the trade unionists, and I did not speak out because I was not a trade unionist. Then they came for the Jews, and I did not speak out because I was not a Jew. Then they came for me and there was no one left to speak for me."

In some ways Martin Niemoller was an unlikely opponent of Nazism because he had fought for Germany during WWI in a U boat, earning the Iron Cross First Class and becoming a hero for his work sinking Allied shipping.

Throughout his earlier life he expressed support for some of the popular fascist ideas of the time. This is not disputed, it's on public record and is an admission he made publicly after the war. He *was* a fascist.

Now before you rush to condemn him too hastily, those same fascist ideas that Niemoller expressed his support for were also very popular and even fashionable in the USA and right across Europe, they were not unique to Germany nor to the Nazi Party, so Niemoller was hardly some 'extreme right winger' by the standards of his day, but the point is that he'd fought for Germany in WWI and was sympathetic to the ideas of the Nazi party in the 1920s and 1930s.

Niemoller had resigned from the German Navy in 1919 in opposition to the Weimar Republic, which was imposed by the victorious Allies onto the defeated Germans. He was vindicated in the worst possible way as hyperinflation of the German Mark due to debt-driven money printing collapsed the economy and caused ever worsening suffering for the German people which Niemoller cared so deeply about.

Given all of this you'd expect the rise of Hitler and the Nazi Party in the 1930s to be celebrated by Niemoller. The ideas of a stable currency, 'jobs for all,' and 'lebensraum' or 'living room' for the German people would surely have appealed to him. Indeed, he voted for the Nazi Party in the 1933 elections which brought Hitler to power.

But Martin Niemoller stands as testament to the fact that a leopard can change its spots. When he saw Hitler in the years after he rose to power he saw clearly what so many of his fellow Lutheran pastors did not. He saw evil.

Even as Hitler became one of the most celebrated figures in history, as Time Magazine's 'Man of the Year,' as the overseer of the spectacular 1936 Olympics, pioneer of the German economic 'miracle' as they emerged at lightning speed from their collapse under the previous Weimar Republic, even as Hitler was admired in the US and the UK and lauded as an example worthy of emulation... despite *all* of this, Niemoller could clearly see the danger that others could not, or perhaps would not, see.

It was Hitler's meddling in the Church which Niemoller initially objected to, with Hitler weaponising the *Deutsche Christen* (German Christian) Protestant faction against all the others and bending them to his will, having them portray Jesus as being Aryan, and teaching that the State ought to be obeyed absolutely, amongst other heresies.

In 1933, the same year that Niemoller voted for Hitler, he founded the Pastors Emergency League and became one of the earliest German pastors to put his objection to Hitler into some sort of action. But it was in January 1934 that Martin Niemoller realised the full extent of the danger that Hitler posed, after a face-to-face meeting with Hitler revealed that Niemoller's phone had been tapped by the Secret Police, that the Pastors Emergency League was being closely monitored by the Gestapo, and that Hitler was going to oppress any church or pastor which did not agree to compromise their theology and acquiesce to Hitler's demands.

After that Niemoller worked tirelessly to raise the alarm, urging the Church to stand up for the faith, with mixed results. There were certainly some courageous pastors during that time, but there was also a great deal of compromise from many churches who preferred power and the favour of the government over the fearless defence of their beliefs, or who chose to simply stay quiet and 'not mix politics and faith.'

Ultimately in 1937 Hitler had had enough of Niemoller's work and he was arrested and imprisoned. Yes, Niemoller was such a thorn in Hitler's side that he was incarcerated two years before the war even began!

He went on to endure eight long years in a concentration camp, suffering greatly but also being sheltered from the war itself. He was freed when the Allies liberated his camp in 1945.

The crucial point to understand here is that everything Hitler did was *legal* according to the courts in Germany, and what Niemoller was doing put him in prison, *legally*.

The German legal system operated under the legal philosophy of 'legal positivism' which I mentioned earlier. It's the view that the government can write any laws it likes and if it is *able* to write and enforce those laws then that's proof that they have the *right* to write and enforce those laws.

This 'legal positivism' stands in stark contrast to the 'rule of law' which we see in the United States, United Kingdom, and throughout the British Empire. The 'rule of law' states that the law is king (Rex Lex) and that there are laws which rule even over kings and queens themselves. This is what's become known as 'common law'—a law that we all have in common, no matter how rich or poor, powerful or powerless.

In the modern world this concept of the 'common law' has morphed uncomfortably and imperfectly into the idea of 'human rights,' being things like the right to life, the right to own and protect your private property, the right to not be punished except if you've been found guilty in a properly run court, etc.

The core idea of 'human rights' is that not even the government has the authority to take them away. These are your rights that stand above the government, these are the *laws above the law*.

As a Christian I believe our rights come from God and are revealed in the Bible. I've already talked about a few of them in this book, and our God-given rights certainly include the right to not be killed for no reason, the right to own and protect our property, the right to trade and do business, the right to be free and move around unrestricted as long as we're not on other people's private property, the right to not be punished unless we've been found guilty of a crime by the testimony of multiple witnesses, and the right to compensation in the event that someone else harms us (which carries the reverse responsibility to make restitution in the event that we harm somebody else).

All these are revealed clearly in Scripture as a part of God's design for the universe, God's law.

The British Empire recognised these truths, these 'laws above the law,' and rejected the idea of legal positivism.

Continental Europe is a very different place to the United Kingdom and the British Empire though, and certainly in Germany 'legal positivism' was practiced by governments and courts alike.

What this means is that Martin Niemoller was, according to the civil authorities, a criminal. He was a law-breaker, defying the lawful rulers of his day and urging others to break the laws which had been passed by the lawful government of the day.

In other words, Pastor Martin Niemoller was defying the civil authorities in violation of Romans 13 and 1 Peter 2 and in most modern churches he would have been called upon to repent for being rebellious...

Except that he wasn't rebellious.

It should be extremely obvious to us all that Martin Niemoller was right to warn against the dangers of Nazism, he was right to object to the Church changing its theology to suit the civil government of the day, and he was right to call for pastors to refuse to comply.

And 1 Peter 2 directly agrees with this because it urges our obedience *for the Lord's sake*.

We are not called to obey the government for the government's sake, nor to obey the law for the law's sake. We are instructed to obey civil authorities *for the Lord's sake*, and this instruction actually applies a *limit* to our obedience! If the purpose of our obedience is for the Lord's sake, what do we do if our obedience is *bad* for the Lord's name?

What if our obedience would cause us to support blasphemy or murder, or anything which is against God's law? In that scenario obedience is no longer *for the Lord's sake*, and in that scenario we *must* obey God and not man!

1 Peter 2 makes it clear that the purpose of our obedience is f*or the Lord's sake, for conscience' sake, and for the purpose of doing good.* If our obedience would actually bring the name of our Lord into disrepute, as some churches did when they complied with Hitler's demands and acquiesced to the German courts, or if our obedience would be a violation of our conscience before God, or if our obedience would in fact cause

us to do bad and *not* good, then the instruction to obey does not apply.

In fact, when man's law and God's law conflict, we must *disobey* man's laws for conscience's sake.

And Martin Niemoller understood this and lived by it, and in his actions we see a man who *did good*, with a *clear conscience*, and brought glory to the *name of Lord Jesus Christ*, by *disobeying* the government.

Now let us shift our focus to a far more controversial example, also from World War II: Dietrich Bonhoeffer.

There is an outstanding and thoroughly comprehensive biography of Dietrich Bonhoeffer authored by Erix Metaxas, titled, *Bonhoeffer: Pastor, Martyr, Prophet, Spy.*

It's not for the fainthearted, at more than six hundred pages!

I'm only going to touch very lightly on the most important, and most controversial, parts of Bonhoeffer's life and work, but if this is enough to whet your appetite and it convinces you to tackle his biography then that's wonderful.

Like Niemoller, Bonhoeffer had spotted by 1933 that Hitler was trouble. Big trouble. Initially, Bonhoeffer's main concern was similar to Niemoller's in the sense that it centred around Hitler's favouring and weaponising of the *Deutsche Christen* sub-denomination to subvert foundational Christian truths, but Bonhoeffer's concerns quickly progressed beyond just the Church and into the wider issue of the state-ordered discrimination against the Jewish people irrespective of their membership of the Church.

Dietrich Bonhoeffer had every reason to ignore his conscience. He was the Student Chaplain at the Charlottenburg Technical College, a well paid and well respected position. He could have consoled himself with the fact that his students needed him and he shouldn't rock the boat—that really these were lofty theological matters for those in positions of high power in the Church. He could have kept his mouth and eyes shut, collected his monthly pay, and let the war pass him by as so many others chose to do.

Bonhoeffer also travelled abroad a great deal and could simply have not returned to Germany. He pastored German-speaking congregations in the UK and travelled many times to speak at symposiums and other events; he had every opportunity and more than enough excuses to simply side-step the controversy and avoid the confrontation altogether, or to keep speaking up but do it from the safety of a foreign land.

But his conscience would not allow him to turn a blind eye. Instead he returned to Germany and defied the German government *for his conscience's sake* in obedience to 1 Peter 2, and ultimately he paid for it with his life.

In April 1933 Bonhoeffer penned an essay for a pastors' meeting. The essay was initially supposed to address the issue of the legal status and recognition of Jewish believers who were baptised into the Church, however his focus shifted radically after the introduction of specific anti-Jew laws, and the Jewish Boycott, where Germans were pressured, shamed, and at times physically intimidated into boycotting Jewish-owned businesses.

After those events Bonhoeffer could no longer restrict his concern just to the theology of his church. He took an extraordinary position against the legitimacy of the laws, and against the legitimacy of the German Government itself.

His essay, titled *Die Kirche vor der Juden frage*, or, *The Church and the Jewish Question*, was so confronting that some of the pastors present in that meeting walked out in protest.

Bonhoeffer argued that the Church had a responsibility to do three key things:

Firstly, they were to question the State injustice—*i.e.*, they were not to keep silent.

Secondly, they were to help the victims of injustice regardless of whether they were members of the Church or not, a fairly radical thought at the time.

But it was his third and final point that proved incendiary: that the Church ought to 'put a spoke in the wheel' of the machinery of oppression and bring it to a halt.

This was an open call for civil disobedience, or worse, for outright resistance and even sedition against the lawfully-elected government of the day. Such a sentiment is dangerous at almost any time or place in history, but it was a life-threatening opinion in Nazi Germany.

It was also heresy to some of the listeners, who had been deceived by the incorrect teaching of Scripture and the fraudulent legal framework of the day, both of which insisted the government could do what it liked and that Christians simply had to obey.

We cannot know what would have happened if Bonhoeffer's call to action had been met with widespread support and if the churches and Christians of Germany had really stood up in early 1934 on behalf of the oppressed against the oppression of the Nazi regime. What we *do* know is that whatever would have come from such Church-led civil disobedience, it could not have been worse than what actually happened thanks to the Church's cowardice.

What if, instead of heeding the shallow interpretation of Romans 13 and 1 Peter 2, which in truth was just a theological veneer for their cowardice, all the churches of Germany had instead heeded Psalm 94 and declared that "Crooked leaders cannot be our friends, because they use the law to cause suffering"? And what if they had also declared that the Government had no power to dictate theology and that it was to be a servant, not an idol?

Would this have been better or worse 'for the sake of the Lord's name'? Would this have been better or worse for their conscience? Would this have caused them to do evil, or would in fact their *disobedience* to the government have been 'doing good' and putting to silence the ignorance of foolish men?

You be the judge, but for me the answer is clear.

Sadly that's not what happened. What happened is that some of the attendees at that meeting where Bonhoeffer argued that the Church should 'put a spoke in the wheel' of injustice actually left in protest, and most of the German Church went on to be silent in the face of rapidly growing Nazi oppression, with some churches openly supporting the government, and very few churches or pastors having the courage to publicly oppose the Nazi regime.

Bonhoeffer was instrumental in the 'Confessing Church,' a movement of churches which directly defied the government-dictated theology of the *Deutsche Christen* 'official' Church, and thank God for the courageous pastors of the Confessing Church who stand as eternal proof that not all pastors or Christians were deceived by the Nazi propaganda, and not everyone was willing to compromise their faith for the sake of a comfortable or prosperous life!

The noose slowly tightened around Bonhoeffer, who trained new pastors in an 'illegal' seminary until it was shut down by the Gestapo in 1937. Even this did not deter Bonhoeffer, who travelled around Germany secretly, continuing to train his students after the seminary was shut down.

The Gestapo were well aware of his activities and began to restrict him more and more, banning him from travel to Berlin in 1938 and banning him from speaking publicly in 1940.

It was in the late 1930s when Bonhoeffer had his first fateful encounter with the anti-Hitler resistance in Germany.

It's worth reading a full biography on Dietrich Bonhoeffer, because the story is quite incredible, but in brief Bonhoeffer's brother-in-law helped him avoid having to fight for the Nazi regime by getting him a role in the Ministry of Intelligence.

Bonhoeffer, true to form, used that role to aid in the resistance, helping to smuggle Jews out of Germany and helping to get information out to the wider world about the atrocities which were beginning to occur.

It's important to remember that no one knew in advance just how horrific things were going to become. No one knew in advance that Hitler was going to implement his barbaric 'Final Solution,' this was something they learned in real-time as they watched it unfold.

Hitler actually tried to deport the Jewish people to the USA, amongst other strategies, to 'fix' the 'Jewish problem,' before resorting to the Holocaust. I don't say this to defend Hitler in any way, but it's important perspective to help us understand the reality for Germans such as Bonhoeffer as they watched in real-time the previously unimaginable horrors unfolding before their eyes.

We read history books about the events, but we already know what's going to happen and so it's easy to judge and say people should have done more. But *they* didn't know, and so it took a remarkable amount of moral clarity and insight for someone like a Bonhoeffer to stand up the way he did and see so far in advance the depth of evil that Hitler would unleash.

Bonhoeffer used his trusted position within the Ministry of Intelligence to help smuggle Jews out and to help warn the world of the emerging atrocities as they happened.

It was when the Gestapo discovered 'Operation Seven,' a resistance plot to get Jews out of Germany, that Bonhoeffer and others were arrested in 1943.

Then on 20 July 1944 there was a coup attempt against Hitler, involving an attempted assassination of Hitler and take-over of the government by Bonhoeffer's resistance colleagues.

The attempt failed and the following investigation revealed the depth of the resistance movement and how deeply it had infiltrated the organs of the German State, including the Ministry of Intelligence. The full extent of Dietrich Bonhoeffer's complicity was revealed in that investigation, including the fact that he had advocated for the assassination of Hitler and, prior to his 1943 arrest, had been complicit in the plans for what became the 1944 failed assassination attempt.

This was a man who had truly 'walked the talk' and done what he could to put a 'spoke in the wheel' of the murderous German war and Holocaust machine, up to and including assisting in the plotting of an assassination.

With his 'crimes' against the murderous Nazi State revealed, Bonhoeffer was moved to the Flossenburg concentration camp, and on 9 April 1945 he was hanged.

Just twenty-one days later Adolf Hitler committed suicide, and twenty-eight days after Bonhoeffer was hanged Germany signed their surrender and the war in Europe was over.

Bonhoeffer died twenty-eight days before he would have seen freedom. Does that mean he failed?

Of course not.

He was faithful, he obeyed God rather than man, and he went home to enjoy his reward in Heaven, which is more than can be said for many of the pastors who opposed or ignored him.

In life he was scorned, rejected, criticised, betrayed, hunted, imprisoned, and executed.

And then he went home and heard the voice of God saying, "Well done, you good and faithful servant."

Bonhoeffer also left a legacy of insightful and challenging wisdom which lives on to this day. You may be familiar with his famous quote:

"Silence in the face of evil is evil itself. Not to speak is to speak, not to act is to act."

He knew well what he was talking about, he'd seen the silence of much of the German Church first-hand.

Less known, but in my opinion even more insightful, is the following:

"Christianity stands or falls with its revolutionary protest against violence, arbitrariness and pride of power, and with its plea for the weak. Christians are doing too little to make these points clear, rather than too much. Christendom adjusts itself far too easily to the worship of power. Christians should give more offence, shock the world far more, than they are doing now."

The legacy of the life he lived continues to this day and we see in his life and his obedience to God's word and to his conscience an example of how we all should live when it is our government that is 'using the law to cause suffering.'

But he didn't do it to set an example for us. He didn't do it so he would be remembered. He did it so that he would have a *clear conscience before God*, so that he would *do good* in accordance with 1 Peter 2, and he did it for the *Lord's sake*.

In other words, he complied with Romans 13 and 1 Peter 2 even as he applied Psalm 94 and disobeyed the civil authorities up to and including plotting an assassination in order to bring an end to the death and suffering Hitler was causing, because those civil authorities were violating their God-given purpose and had stepped outside of their God-given authority.

Martin Niemoller and Dietrich Bonhoeffer are by no means the only examples of Christian civil disobedience *for the Lord's sake*, but they stand as two particularly shining examples during a particularly dark time in history, and they were both men with sincere faith whose *disobedience* to civil authorities was motivated by their faith and faithfulness to God in accordance with Scripture.

Utopia Revisited

Unhappily, the worst of the Nazi atrocities are not as far in the past as you think, and it would be remiss of me not to talk about why.

There is a reason why I've used so many examples from the Nazi regime in both my books. It's because the exact same evil that was at work in the Nazi regime is still at work in our nations today, and the Church is failing again.

And I'm not directly speaking of the sharp return of antisemitism which we've seen since 2021, although that's certainly a concern; I'm speaking of the fact that for millennia man has justified doing evil against our fellow man on the basis of racial or genetic superiority, and that with gene editing and genetic vaccines now becoming a reality, that ancient evil is returning in a new form.

The Church failed this test once already in my lifetime, so please allow me to devote this chapter to explaining what we face, where it's come from, and what to watch for so that hopefully the Church will never fail it again.

Racism is nothing new. The idea that one race of people is superior to another has existed in one form or another since Creation, and this is *not* a white versus black issue—almost every racial group has believed itself to be superior at some point in history, and quite a few still do now, including Brahman in India and various people groups in Africa. Indeed, if you want an object lesson in racism, be a fly on the wall while one group of Asians talks about the others... it doesn't matter which group you listen to, you'll hear all about how inferior all the other groups are.

Racism is as old as time, and we have records of race-based atrocities and genocides taking place thousands of years ago, as well as records of families refusing to marry into specific racial groups, and records of certain tribes and families enslaving others purely on the basis of their own 'superiority.'

And it's not just the 'white on black' issue that is portrayed today. There's a long and violent history of the black Barbary Coast Pirates who used to capture and enslave white people into the African continent, and the history of how claimed racial superiority led to slavery in China, Japan, Korea, Egypt, Mongolia, Babylon, and every other ancient empire.

It's racist of you to think that only the white races are capable of racism!

For thousands of years racism was practised simply because of the physical differences between people groups, tribes, and families. It was considered a 'fact,' for example, that Romans were superior to the Germanic people, that the Chinese were superior to their neighbouring races, that (in the West) white people were superior to black, and that (in Africa) black people were superior to white.

The 'Slavic' people groups in Eastern Europe are called 'Slavs' because they were, for many centuries, taken into slavery by raiders from Africa and elsewhere, often becoming slaves for people with far darker skin than theirs.

Racism and slavery in history was not a 'one way' problem, it was a free-for-all in which every human group was certain of their own superiority over the others. This seems to be a near-universal symptom of the fallen nature of mankind. The British Empire was the first in recorded history to abolish slavery, but that didn't end the racism and 'superiority' complex so deeply ingrained in human nature; it simply caused it to morph.

Our fallen nature cannot be fixed by human forces. No amount of enlightenment, knowledge, research, or science can fix the human heart. So it should not surprise us that right around the same time as race-based slavery was being put to an end in the British Empire, racism found a new cloak to wear and a new way to sell itself: Science.

The scientific method has brought tremendous good to the world, however the principle of 'garbage in, garbage out' remains true in science as much as it does elsewhere.

When someone simply applies a veneer of 'science' to their pre-existing prejudices it leads to terrible things.

In this case, the 'someone' in question was Charles Darwin.

Darwin was part of a wider 'naturalistic' movement which was popular in his day. It sought to find answers to all the questions of life, the universe, and everything, in the natural world around us. They wanted to explain it all without needing God.

Naturalists believed that life had natural, rather than divine, origin, and that science and scientists would be the new truth-tellers, the new clergy (not that they put it in those terms) in a new religion in which God was dead.

It was a journey to the far side of the earth on the ship *Beagle* that brought Charles Darwin to the Galapagos Islands, where he made his observations about the unique physical characteristics of some of the birds there.

Out of this journey he wrote his seminal work, *The Origin of the Species.*

Except, that's not the full title. The full original title is:

On the Origin of the Species by Means of Natural Selection, or the Preservation of the Favoured Races in the Struggle for Life.

Yes, that's right, racism and the idea of "favoured" (superior) "races" was central to Darwin's world view and his world-changing work.

Darwin's book rapidly became wildly popular with the mostly-white, mostly-wealthy 'science' establishment of his day, because of course it did. It appealed to the fallen nature of mankind and gave a veneer of scientific respectability with which to assert their 'obvious' racial superiority as white people who, Darwin posited, were more 'evolved' away from their ape 'ancestors' than darker-coloured people.

This was before there was any direct understanding of genetics. The cell was very poorly understood, and DNA would have blown their minds.

None of these men knew what they *didn't* know or just how ignorant they were of the phenomenal complexity of life within every living cell, but that didn't matter. Thanks to the work of Charles Darwin they suddenly had a 'scientific' basis for their racism and they could justify their sinful sense of superiority, so they lapped it up.

I'm simplifying, of course, but I would sum up that era of the emergence and popularisation of *natural* origins for life and the universe as the era of Romans 1:18-25:

For the wrath of God is revealed from heaven against all ungodliness and unrighteousness of men who suppress the truth in unrighteousness, because that which is known about God is evident within them; for God made it evident to them. For since the creation of the world His invisible attributes, His eternal power and divine nature, have been clearly seen, ***being understood through what has been made****, so that they are without excuse. For even though they knew God, they did not honour Him as God or give thanks, but* ***they became futile in their speculations****, and their foolish heart was darkened.*

Professing themselves to be wise, they became fools, and exchanged the glory of the incorruptible God for an image in the form of corruptible man and of birds and four-footed animals and crawling creatures.

Therefore God gave them over in the lusts of their hearts to impurity, so that their bodies would be dishonoured among them. ***For they exchanged the truth of God for a lie, and worshipped and served the creature rather than the Creator****, who is blessed forever. Amen.*

This passage addresses actual idolatry, the worship of physical idols in the form of animals, but I believe it also speaks directly about the Creator God being replaced by natural origins, replaced by animals which evolved and changed and 'became our creator.'

Verse 23 says that man would "exchange the glory of the incorruptible God for an image in the form of corruptible man and of birds and four-footed animals and crawling creatures," and if that isn't a perfect description of naturalism and Darwin's theory of evolution then I don't know what is.

Darwinism is idolatry, a worshipping of the creature rather than the Creator. But like all idolatry it appealed to the deepest parts of the fallen human heart, and in this case it gave the *appearance* of respectability to the racism and superiority complex which mankind harbours.

Suddenly it was respectable to assert racial superiority again—now you could explain, using the latest, most modern, most *scientific* explanations, exactly *why* you were superior.

Out of this scientifically justified superiority was born the Eugenics movement.

Before we get to Eugenics, it's worth noting that by the end of Charles Darwin's life the most advanced understanding of biology, the most 'cutting edge science,' still viewed the cell as really very simple.

Darwin did speak of the 'complexity' of the cell by citing the most advanced research of the day, which was a paper published by Mr G. H. Lewes in the *Fortnightly Review*, 1 Nov 1868. Although Darwin does use the word 'complex' to describe the cell—and that would have made sense, because he had no idea how complex a cell would *really* turn out to be—the paper upon which Darwin relies is cartoonishly simple, supposing the cell to have a few basic parts made up mostly of membranes and 'jelly-like substances.'

There was no understanding of DNA and RNA or proteins and protein folding—all the astounding processes which take place within the 'jelly-like substances' in our cells.

More than a hundred years later, the cell was described by Bruce Alberts, the former US Academy of Sciences President, as "a factory that contains an elaborate network of interlocking assembly lines, each of which is composed of a set of large protein machines." There's an estimated thirty *trillion* cells in the human body, each running this "network of interlocking assembly lines" composed of "large protein machines."

The human brain alone is believed to contain more than eighty billion neurons which, if laid end to end, would wrap around the earth's equator more than twelve times. These cells are all contained within your skull and joined by over one hundred *trillion* connections that allow you to function, think, imagine, love, and even decide that there is no God and that all of this is just a cosmic accident.

That whole astonishing arrangement of brain matter, doing all of its amazing and complex computing, runs on less power than an old incandescent light bulb, or about 20W.

But Darwin didn't know any of that, nor did he know what he didn't know. From his perspective, he was at the cutting edge of 'science,' and with his theory of evolution via mutation and natural selection he had theorised away the 'need' for a creator and replaced Him with aeons of time, mutation via gemmules (a now-discredited theory by which he tried to explain the effect of what we now know to be genes), and natural selection (or the death of the weak), leading to the 'survival of the fittest,' the emergence of more and more complex life-forms, and ultimately more and more 'superior' races of humans.

It was ignorance and arrogance, foolishness professing itself to be wisdom. It was idolatry, trading God and His design for animals and death. But the world ignorantly and foolishly adopted this new, 'scientific' world view, and some quickly began to take the theory of evolution to its logical conclusion.

If you start by rejecting God and accept purely naturalistic origins for life, a few things immediately become apparent:

1. Without God life has no meaning or value of itself. Therefore there's nothing wrong with killing.
2. If the death of the 'inferior races' is necessary for the emergence of the 'superior' ones (natural selection in a nutshell), what's to stop us 'helping' by killing off the 'inferior' races faster?

And so the Eugenics movement was born. Eugenics was very popular and even fashionable throughout the Western world. It was completely acceptable in high-society to support Eugenics, and many 'charities' sprung up to help put Eugenics into practice.

Inter-racial marriages had long been frowned upon because of the aforementioned 'superiority' many people feel about themselves, but Darwin gave these ideas a new veneer of scientific validity.

There's truly nothing new under the sun, only new labels for old things. Eugenics took the place of racism.

In the name of Eugenics people with intellectual disabilities were sterilised against their will to stop them from breeding, for the 'greater good' of course!

And such acts had a 'scientific' respectability and virtue which made Eugenics a noble cause, an acceptable charity, a virtuous field to study.

Sadly even many churches bought in to the Eugenics lie, without necessarily adopting wholeheartedly all of Darwin's theory. They took the bits that suited them, such as white superiority over black people on the basis that black people were presumed to be closer to being apes than were white people, and left out the rest.

They 'kept' God, whilst rejecting His created order in which all mankind is equal before Him.

So whilst slavery on the basis of race might have been abolished from the British Empire, and later from the United States of America, racism was alive and well and more respectable than ever thanks to Eugenics!

In the early 1900s Margaret Sanger, the founder of Planned Parenthood, rose to prominence. She was a Eugenicist who stated in 1921, "The most urgent problem today is how to limit and discourage the over-fertility of the mentally and physically defective."

Sanger wanted human abortion to be available on demand, and was actually opposed by other Eugenicists who feared that the 'more educated' (*i.e.* white) women would be more likely to kill their babies, which would then have the opposite effect to what the Eugenicists wanted!

But Sanger understood this 'problem' and focused her efforts on minority, and particularly black, communities in the South, targeting those whom Eugenicists argued were 'inferior.'

In 1939 Sanger wrote a letter discussing her plan to get church leaders to stop accusing her of racism, "We do not want word to go out that we want to exterminate the Negro population, and the minister is the man who can straighten out that idea if it ever occurs to any of their more rebellious members."

There is legitimate debate about whether this sentence is an admission that she really *did* want to exterminate the black population, or if she was merely addressing the accusations levelled against her.

In 2014 a study found that 40% of Planned Parenthood locations are in majority-black communities, even though black people make up only 13% of the US population, a three times over-representation of abortion clinics in black communities.

Is that for the purpose of 'serving' them with 'healthcare,' or for the purpose of reducing their reproduction rate and eliminating a race that Sanger deemed inferior based on her Darwinian Eugenics ideas?

You be the judge.

Ultimately it was Eugenics that led to Hitler's 'Final Solution' for the Jews both directly *and* indirectly.

Directly, because Eugenics informed Hitler's ideas about the 'superior' Aryan race and the need for a 'solution' for the 'Jewish problem'—*i.e.*, that the Jewish people were an inferior race and needed to be eliminated from the gene pool; and indirectly, because Eugenics also contributed to US President Roosevelt's anti-Jewish sentiment and his failure to accept and encourage Jewish refugees from Europe at a time when they might have been saved.

The story of President Roosevelt is complex, and whilst it can be argued that he 'did what he could' within the constraints he faced, the fact remains that up until 1942 the Nazi regime would have happily deported the Jews to anyone who would take them, a fact that Roosevelt was well aware of, and he simply didn't want to allow them into the United States.

I did mention it earlier, but it's been largely forgotten in popular culture that the Nazis actually made considerable efforts to deport the Jews before resorting to exterminating them in 1942. They explored options such as mass deportations to Africa or anywhere which would take them, but various plans were thwarted for logistical reasons, and when all else had failed, the barbaric 'Final Solution' was implemented.

And to repeat myself, that is not a defence or justification for Nazi atrocities and the Holocaust. The Jewish people should have been left entirely in peace and treated exactly the same as every other human being, and none of the history that I'm pointing out here should be interpreted as saying otherwise!

But I believe it's important to point out this detail from history because there were *many* opportunities for the Western powers to save the victims of the Holocaust before it happened, and we *didn't do it*, in part because our leaders had accepted Eugenics and they didn't want the 'Jewish problem,' as they saw it, to be imported into their countries.

Support for Eugenics collapsed after WWII, thanks to the horror people felt at seeing it taken to its logical conclusion in Nazi death camps.

It used to be astonishing to me that people needed to see it in action to realise what a horrific and barbaric belief Eugenics was, but since Covid I understand how it happened, and how it will happen again.

Once the world saw what Eugenics really meant in the Nazi ideology, support for it evaporated and we entered a time of historic peace and unprecedented racial harmony.

Yes, really.

By objective measures, the seventy-five years following the end of WWII has been astonishingly peaceful globally, and it has also been a rare period in history when racial relations and tensions decreased.

These tensions didn't disappear, of course, but the world was so horrified by the full outworking of racism in the Holocaust that, bit by bit, a host of racist laws were ended and, at least in the West, the culture shifted from one that celebrated racism to one that rejected it.

Segregation ended in the US, Apartheid ended in South Africa, and expressing racism publicly became frowned upon. Racist jokes were still told, and racist insults were still used, but they were used by the outliers rather than the leaders. Being found telling such jokes or giving such insults would lead to rejection or correction by the culture at large, where such jokes used to be celebrated.

Racism was certainly not gone, but in comparison to almost any other time in history, it was greatly diminished.

By the time I was born in Australia in 1982, public awareness campaigns to 'say no to racism' were commonplace, and by the late 1980s the idea that any of us would tease our school classmates for their ethnicity was out of the question entirely; we would be punished by other kids in the playground, and by teachers and the principal in his office, if we did.

I'm not saying the world was perfect or that there was *no* racism, far from it, but it's a *fact* that by historical standards we had three quarters of a century of relative peace internationally and relative peace interracially.

But it was never going to last.

There is a saying that "Those who do not learn from history are doomed to repeat it." That's true, but sadly those of us who *do* learn from history are doomed to watch helplessly as those who do *not* learn from history repeat it despite our attempts to warn them!

And although history never repeats exactly, it certainly rhymes, and the next stanza of the long, sad, and sorry history of discrimination on the basis of supposed racial or genetic 'superiority' has begun in earnest.

When slavery ended as one form of 'superiority,' Darwinian Eugenics replaced it. When that ended, something was always going to take its place.

This time the 'superiority' is not in our inherited DNA or the genes we get from our parents. This time the 'superiority' comes specifically via the human augmentation of our DNA.

The new 'superiority,' the new 'elite,' are those whose DNA has been augmented by human intervention. It's already started and 90% of the population didn't even notice.

It started with the Covid mRNA jabs.

Where humans of the past have asserted their superiority on the basis of their naturally inherited characteristics—skin colour, height, intellect, etc.—in this new era of gene editing and mRNA jabs discrimination is emerging on the basis of who has, or has not, been augmented.

No, this isn't some sci-fi fantasy about what will happen in the future. On the contrary, it's very real, it's already happened once, and the vast majority of people, and most of the Church, went along with it.

Governments in Australia and around the world placed restrictions on anyone who refused to participate in the global trial of the mRNA Covid jabs on the basis that those who had not been augmented were a danger to those who had.

Rules were passed denying mRNA jab-refusers entry into pubs and clubs, cinemas and sporting events, weddings, funerals, and churches and synagogues.

And overwhelmingly, churches around the world complied.

The parallels to mid 1930s Germany placing increasing restrictions on Jews, and increasingly using legal and social pressure against Germans who did not join them in discriminating against Jews, should be obvious.

No, of course I'm not comparing Covid medical segregation to the Holocaust 'Final Solution' which ran from 1942 till 1945; that would be a preposterous comparison. But I *am* comparing Covid segregation to the 1933-1939 campaign to marginalise, dehumanise, and stigmatise the Jewish people.

It was the *fear of disease* which was wielded as a primary weapon against the Jews from 1933 to 1939. There was a typhus pandemic at the time and the Jews were blamed by the government for being the cause of the spread.

They were the unclean, the disease-spreaders, the granny killers of their day, and *that* is why they 'had' to be ostracised, shunned, and avoided. Disease was the spectre the government used to ensure the people complied and even helped as they marginalised the genetically 'inferior.' Still can't see the parallels to Covid and the unjabbed?

The Covid restrictions took a variety of forms but in them all the message was clear: the unjabbed are unclean, disease-spreaders, and granny killers.

Churches around the world rolled over in meek obedience to government orders to segregate their congregation on the basis of who had accepted the lordship of the government over their body and immune system and allowed their genes to be 'augmented,' those who had allowed their immune system to be 'patched' like a software program, at the government's orders.

Our God-given human genetics, our God-given DNA 'fingerprint,' unique to every human being, was no longer good enough to get basic human rights.

We were all now subject to regular 'patches,' mandatory updates to our 'anti-virus program' via man-made mRNA injections. Human genetics was reduced to the plaything of the government and discrimination on the basis of genetics came rushing back into vogue.

The Eugenics of the early 1900s made a comeback in the 2020s, again given the veneer of scientific validity, and garnished with the urgency of a 'once in a lifetime pandemic' to help frighten people into fear and compliance.

This new technology that allows us to directly edit human DNA and switch genes on or off opens up exciting new possibilities for the future of medicine, but also opens up a new way for governments to create 'utopia' and for humans to assert superiority.

Consider that the Germans promised a superior race, a new turbo-charged era of evolutionary development leading to a race of 'super humans,' if only they could inbreed the 'good' and weed out the 'bad.'

It's sometimes forgotten that the Nazi regime did not only try to exterminate the Jews, along with Gypsies and some blacks as well, but that they also had forced breeding programs of tall, white, blonde people in an effort to fast-track the evolution of the 'ideal' 'Aryan' race.

The Nazis did not believe they were committing acts of unspeakable evil. They believed they were creating a new utopia, filled with stronger, smarter, 'better' humans, and that their atrocities would be recognised by future generations as visionary, wonderful, necessary, and good.

The same idea of breeding a superior people underpinned the British exiling of the 'criminal class,' as I've mentioned already. By getting rid of these 'inferiors' and leaving the British Isles to be populated only by 'fit and proper persons,' they were creating an island paradise... or so they thought.

It's the promise of utopia. It's *always* the promise of utopia. And utopia is always just a few more killings, deportations, or exilings away.

Governments are trying to take God's place, and so they must create Heaven on Earth. And heaven is just a few more rules, a few more taxes, a few more restrictions, or a few more executions away.

I recall my growing sense of horror as I watched the media and even some politicians call for ever-harsher restrictions on those of us who chose not to get the Covid jabs.

Actual government policies included segregation of the unjabbed from shops, work places, and public venues. As one small example, I was unable to enter a large retailer in order to buy my son a pushbike for his birthday, because I did not have a 'Covid pass' green tick on my phone proving I was double-jabbed.

I had to stand outside and wait for a staff member to bring out the box after I bought and paid for it online on my phone while standing in front of the store. I was not allowed to approach the employee, I had to stand back until they had deposited the box and walked away, scurrying to a 'safe' distance with a mask over their face, gloves on their hands, and fear in their eyes. No, I'm not making this up. I had no illness, no symptoms whatsoever. I wasn't sick at all, and this employee was presumably at least double-jabbed, but despite being 'protected' by the mRNA jabs themself, plus a mask and gloves, this grown adult was absolutely freaking terrified of me, a completely healthy fellow human being, because the TV told them I was 'unclean.'

All so I could give my son a birthday present.

It's hard to believe it till you experience it yourself, but once you've lived it you can't unsee the parallels to 1930s Germany.

On another occasion I had to seek out an 'illegal hair cut' because as one of the 'unclean' I was not legally allowed to get my hair cut in my home state of Victoria. The fact that a haircut could be considered 'illegal' in a liberal democracy should be all the proof you need that we had lost our minds.

In my home city of Melbourne, Australia, the police used to enter weddings and funerals to demand proof from all attendees that they were vaccinated in compliance with the rules at the time. The lack of sensitivity and sheer bloody-mindedness required to think this was acceptable should be shocking, but it's not. It was 'normal' for over a year, and if you objected then *you* were the problem.

And pastors, elders, and police officers, all grown adult human beings, went along with it willingly, and some of them went along with it with *enthusiasm* to show their obedience to the idol of government and cement their place in the new 'superior' overclass.

Those Covid restrictions I've mentioned are just a small sample of the actual restrictions which were enforced on the unjabbed, but they pale into nothing when compared to what some in the media and politics actually wanted.

Over the course of 2021 and early 2022 I watched prominent people in the media call for all manner of human rights violations including ongoing indefinite house-arrest for the unjabbed, forced vaccinations against our will, and even for the unjabbed to be incarcerated in camps, literal concentration camps (though that's not what they called them) to 'protect' the 'good' and 'safe' people from us 'unclean' sub-humans.

No, those proposals were not seriously considered by those in power, and again I'm not comparing the Covid madness with the actual Holocaust, but it is telling that it was *more socially acceptable to publicly call for concentration camps than it was to refuse to participate in the mRNA jab experiment.*

You *could* post online that the unjabbed should be locked up in camps, but you *couldn't* post online that the unjabbed should protest against the restrictions.

I know that because I was prosecuted for the latter, but no one has ever been prosecuted (nor should they be, I believe free speech should be absolute) for the former.

Every genocide in history is preceded by a campaign to dehumanise the future victims. The campaign to dehumanise jab refusers was real, devastatingly effective, and all on the pseudo-scientific basis of our supposed inferiority, this time because we had not been genetically augmented by the latest and greatest medical innovations.

This is the new frontier of superiority, segregation, and future genocide. Once upon a time racism, oppression, slavery, and genocide was justified on the basis of obvious physical differences, then after Darwin's theory and the rise of Eugenics they were justified on the basis on presumed genetic 'inferiority,' and now we are arriving at a new reality where oppression is justified on the basis of artificial genetic augmentation and man-made genetic 'superiority.'

It's the same sin with a new label, and that's not a prediction for the future, it's already happened and most of the Church went along with it and even celebrated it.

It's the inevitable consequence of our idolatry.

In Covid we got off lightly. The oppression and dehumanising of the unjabbed, the un-augmented, never reached its full, horrific, logical conclusion of genocide like it did in 1930s Germany, or in the killing fields of Cambodia, or like is happening right now in parts of Africa.

So yes, it could have been worse, but is that really the measure we want to use? We should all be horrified at just how far we went, and just how quickly we got there, and just how much the Church complied.

Because those who do not learn from history...

A Clash of World-Views

What we are seeing today is a continuation of the direct clash between good and evil, God and Satan, Heaven and Hell which has been raging since Satan the Archangel fell from Heaven, taking a third of the angels with him.

God is pro-Human. He loves us, He created the universe for our habitation, He gave us dominion over all of His creation.

Satan hates God, and hates everything that God loves. Which means Satan hates us. Satan is anti-human.

Ever since Satan fell he has been trying to destroy the pinnacle of God's creation: Mankind.

In Genesis 1:28 God instructed mankind,

"Be fruitful and multiply; fill the earth and subdue it; have dominion over the fish of the sea, over the birds of the air, and over every living thing that moves on the earth."

This is very different to his earlier instructions to animals to 'fill the earth.' He never told animals to 'subdue' the earth or to have 'dominion' over the earth; that's an instruction He only gave to humans.

The word 'subdue' in the original Hebrew is '*kabosh*,' which literally means to 'cultivate' or to make it 'yield service to' the one who is doing the subduing.

God is literally instructing humans to fill and subdue the wild forces of our planet for the purpose of making the earth more serviceable and comfortable for us, humans.

This planet and all the resources it provides are entrusted by God to us as stewards—these resources are a gift from God, for us to *use*, to change and terraform and cultivate the planet and make it *yield service* to us.

Now, to be clear, we are *stewards* of the earth, not owners. Only God is the owner of the earth, just as God is the owner of each of us. But it was God's idea to make us the stewards and it was His idea to give us all the resources on the earth and the instructions to *subdue* it.

As *stewards* we have a responsibility to use the earth's resources wisely and to pass the planet to our children *better* than it was when it was given to us, so being told to 'subdue' is not permission to be irresponsible or reckless or leave behind scorched earth, but it is *also* not permission to simply leave it alone and not change it at all.

This comes back once again to the Bible's instruction, "A righteous man leaves an inheritance to his children's children," and that inheritance must include a natural environment *and* a built environment that is suited to living and living well. I'm not advocating strip-mining the planet or recklessly polluting it in pursuit of temporary hedonistic pleasure—that would be a betrayal of future generations and a failure to leave them an inheritance—but God is absolutely clear that this planet is ours to *subdue*, to make *better for us and for our descendants*, and we should not feel guilty about making this planet *better* for humans, *easier* for us to live and survive and thrive on.

God makes it clear that *He is pro-human* in his intentions for us on this earth. The earth is entrusted to us to use and change and plough and mine and *put into service* to make *human lives,* our lives *and* the lives of our descendants, better.

This contrasts sharply with the anti-human world view of the so-called humanists, who whether they know it or not are actually worshipping Satan.

Humanism declares that God is dead, there is no God, and that by default therefore humans are the ultimate authority in the universe.

On paper you'd think that humanism is 'pro-human,' that it elevates humanity higher, but nothing could be further from the truth.

By rejecting God's created order and God's design for humanity as the stewards and masters of the earth, humanism has diminished the human race into a mere cosmic accident and, worse, a virus on the face of the earth.

The idea that humans are a virus that is overpopulating the earth and heading for an inevitable disastrous collapse has been around for some time. It's known as 'Malthusianism' because it was popularised by British author Thomas Robert Malthus in the late 1700s.

Malthus' book, much like Darwin's *Origin of Species* which was published half a century later, had an immediate effect and was widely read and believed among the wealthier upper-class members of British society.

And like Darwin's later work, Malthus appealed to the sense of superiority of some humans over others, a superiority which British 'society' already felt in their core and were only too happy to 'validate' by reading and believing books such as his.

Malthus contributed to the idea that heaven on earth can be created if you just eliminate the inferior and replace them with the 'superior,' and he went further, by suggesting that a *failure* to do so would lead to *hell on earth*.

This is clearly shown in the full title of T. R. Malthus' essay: *An Essay on the Principle of Population; or, a View of its Past and Present Effects on Human Happiness; with an Inquiry into* ***our Prospects Respecting the Future Removal or Mitigation of the Evils which it Contains***.

It is assumed in this essay that the human population contains evils which must be removed or mitigated.

This was published at a time when slavery was still rife across the British Empire and the superiority of the British man over all other strains of humanity was considered self-evident (by the British men, of course).

Malthus warned that the food supply would not keep up with population growth, resources would run out, and a future apocalypse and collapse of civilisation would occur unless population growth was kept under control.

Which population must be kept down? Well, not the superior British white man of course!

These ideas are alive and well in our culture. Malthus' ideas can be seen in the 1968 best-selling book by Paul Ehrlich, *The Population Bomb*, which predicted global famines due to overpopulation—famines which never came to pass, even as the population far exceeded Ehrlich's predictions.

Malthusianism reared its head again in a 1972 report by the Club of Rome, titled *Limits to Growth*.

This was a computer-modelling study of five areas where they predicted humans would reach the limits of the earth's carrying capacity—*i.e.*, the limit of how much the earth could be 'subdued' in accordance with Genesis 1, and that famine and population collapse would follow in the near future.

These five areas were: Population, Food Production, Non-renewable resources (such as mined resources), industrial production, and pollution.

The predictions were apocalyptic... and they were also very wrong, just like Ehrlich's 'Population Bomb' was wrong.

But people took them very seriously at the time, and still do to this day, and the idea that mankind is a 'virus,' that we're devastating the planet, and that some kind of environmental collapse is inevitable because we've done *too much subduing of the planet*, has successfully taken over the public consciousness despite having been wrong every time so far, *and* despite the fact that the earth is actually in better shape today than it was 250 years ago despite the multiplied human population!

Climate Change is the latest of the scare campaigns, and perhaps the most successful, but like all the scare campaigns that came before it, it's mostly based on nonsense.

The idea is that atmospheric Co2 is a *primary* driver of earth's climate, *and* that mankind's Co2 emissions are tipping the balance in a way that natural forces cannot mitigate, *and* that this will lead to runaway warming of the planet, *and* that this warming will result in an apocalypse of human suffering and eco-system collapse, threatening life on earth as we know it.

Sounds serious!

But never fear! The *government* will save you by taxing you and diminishing your life, restricting your every act to stop you from changing or 'subduing' the earth, including controlling the food you eat, the jobs you work, the travel you enjoy, and whether or not you can heat your home in winter.

Mankind *subduing* the earth is the *problem* you see? God got it wrong, but thankfully we have a new god in the form of government, and they know better.

Never mind that despite breathless headlines to the contrary the predicted apocalypse never appears. Never mind that the earth is in an interglacial period, meaning we're still emerging from an ice age and the earth is *of course* warming slowly and that this warming is both natural *and* expected. Never mind that the earth has been much warmer in history than it is now and that was entirely natural and was actually *good* for life, not bad! Never mind that the effect of the atmosphere on the surface temperature is much more a function of the mass of the gasses in the atmosphere than its chemical composition (look at the Simple Gas Laws for more information on this). Never mind that by every metric the world is in great shape compared to 250 or even 100 years ago—for example, burned area from wildfires is lower, hurricane landfalls are lower, polar bear populations are just fine, and thanks to satellites we know that the surface amount of 'green' (vegetation) on earth is actually increasing, thanks in part to increased atmospheric Co2 making plants more water efficient!

There's actually a lot of good news about our planet today! But good news doesn't sell newspapers, get government grants for more research, or get you elected. Powerful people *need* an apocalypse, and *need* you to believe that only they can save you. It's their god complex at work, and a world that has rejected the one true God is only too happy to replace Him with them.

Why do you think that all the solutions to all our problems involve more power for them, more taxes, and less individual freedom? Why is the solution always that 'we' give up something so that 'they' can save us?

They *need* to be your god, but if they can't deliver utopia, Heaven on Earth, then they'll instead promise to save us from hell on earth... a hell that may exist only in their imagination, but they'll 'save' us anyway. But just as their man-made utopia requires us to live diminished lives and, indeed, for many of us to die, so too does 'saving' us from their imagined hell.

It's almost as if 'heaven' and 'hell' aren't really the point, these are just a vehicle by which they justify their desire to play god and kill a bunch of us off.

The Georgia Guide Stones are an emblem of the problem.

The Georgia Guide Stones were unveiled in 1980, barely a decade after Paul Ehrlich's *Population Bomb* book and the Club of Rome *Limits to Growth* report captured the public consciousness.

A man using the pseudonym of Robert C. Christian had a local Georgia stone mason erect these enormous slabs of granite, inscribed with 'Guiding Principles for Humanity' in eight different languages!

Christian claimed to be acting on behalf of a group of wealthy and powerful people, but he also claimed elsewhere that he alone was responsible for the inscriptions, the 'guiding principles,' which were written on the stones.

No one knows the truth of which people were behind these huge slabs of stone with their ten guiding principles, but by reading the principles we can clearly see which world view, pro-human or anti-human, was behind them.

These 'principles' were:

1. Maintain humanity under 500,000,000 in perpetual balance with nature.
2. Guide reproduction wisely — improving fitness and diversity.
3. Unite humanity with a living new language.
4. Rule passion — faith — tradition — and all things with tempered reason.
5. Protect people and nations with fair laws and just courts.
6. Let all nations rule internally resolving external disputes in a world court.
7. Avoid petty laws and useless officials.
8. Balance personal rights with social duties.
9. Prize truth — beauty — love — seeking harmony with the infinite.
10. Be not a cancer on the earth — Leave room for nature — Leave room for nature.

Even putting aside the fact that ten 'principles' written on slabs of granite is an obvious counterfeit to the Ten Commandments which God wrote on tablets of stone in the Old Testament, even putting aside the fact that the mysterious person behind the project chose the name 'Christian' as his pseudonym despite many of the 'principles' being overtly anti-Christian... even if we just take these ten principles at their word exactly as written and ignore all the other weirdness... we still run immediately into some major red flags.

Let's go through a few key issues.

Principle 1: Maintain humanity under 500,000,000 in perpetual balance with nature.

Even in 1980, when the stones were unveiled, there were nearly 4,500,000,000 people on earth. What should be done with the 'surplus' 4 BILLION people?

That looks like a call to genocide to me, but let's be charitable and say they're not advocating genocide, but rather a dramatic reduction in birth rates and letting natural attrition reduce the population via natural causes.

OK, that still means we're having very few kids, in fact most of us are having *no* kids, and someone has to have the power to enforce that rule on anyone who has too many... China style one-child policies wouldn't even be enough, you'd need something even stricter, enforced by a government even more totalitarian.

Contrast this with God's instruction to be fruitful, multiply, and *fill* the earth, and notice that these stones assume that a population of more than 500,000,000 humans is automatically not 'in harmony with nature.' This is a direct affront to God's instruction to mankind to fill *and* subdue the earth.

Principle 2 gives us a clue as to how this reduction in global population could be achieved: Guide reproduction wisely — improving fitness and diversity.

Yep, that's our old enemy Eugenics rearing its ugly head again. King Solomon was right when he wrote in Ecclesiaste1:9, "What has been will be again, what has been done will be done again; There is nothing new under the sun"!

To 'guide' reproduction in such a way would require some sort of totalitarian state with the power and the will to sterilise the 'unfit' and to match up the 'fit' into breeding pairs. This is nothing short of a call for the return of Nazi 'master race' breeding experiments, and we should all recoil at the thought.

Contrast this again with God's created order, that God has created all men equal, with equal God-given dignity, that He desires relationship with each and every one of us regardless of our perceived 'fitness' in the opinion of others, and that Christ died for *you* because God the Father wants to be reconciled with you irrespective of your genetics, race, health, intellect, or abilities.

It's fallen man that judges others by those metrics, but God looks at the human heart, and each and every one of us has one of those. God gave you one Himself.

And so we see that God is more pro-human than the humanists are.

Principle 4 should concern us all: Rule passion — faith — tradition — and all things with tempered reason.

That may sound like a great idea but it inherently requires that we place a human authority over the top of our faith. Our faith, our traditions, our 'passion,' must be made subject to human authorities that will 'rule' these things with 'tempered reason.'

The movie *Equilibrium* springs to mind, a dystopian post-apocalyptic film about a world with a totalitarian government which has outlawed emotion. The government has decided to create 'utopia' by outlawing the source of all murder, crime, and war: emotions.

Citizens are forced to take daily doses of a drug that suppresses their emotions, and a ruthless police force hunts down and destroys anything that might trigger emotions: music, art, poetry, and anything or anyone that might cause passion to rise in the human heart must be destroyed, and the people responsible must be 'processed,' a euphemism for being exterminated.

Yes, it's a B-grade science-fiction film, but the observations it makes about human nature and the lust for power are spot on. The government plays god and pursues a counterfeit vision of a man-made utopia complete with exterminations and oppression 'for your own good,' and in the process that government destroys all the good gifts that the true God has given us, including our passion, art, love, and connection.

But back to the Guidestones. Most of these 'principles' are deeply concerning, but I think I've made my point, so let me jump to the final one.

Principle 10: Be not a cancer on the earth — Leave room for nature — Leave room for nature.

This is as anti-human a sentiment as you can imagine, and explicitly contradicts God's created design.

Our *use* of the planet was God's idea, our multiplying and filling the earth was His instruction, and our taking dominion and subduing the earth, changing the earth to suit our needs and provide a better life to our descendants, was his design for how we would leave an inheritance to our children's children.

The idea of leaving 'room for nature' is rampant in our politics today. National Parks, which once were supposed to preserve the natural environment so that humans could enter and enjoy it with bushwalking, rock climbing, camping, fishing, and hunting, are now being locked up so that humans cannot enter them at all.

We've culturally accepted the idea that humans 'spoil' nature just by existing in it, that an 'untouched' natural environment is always better than something humans have altered—even if it can be objectively shown that humans have made something better for plants and animals as well as for themselves.

'Rewilding' an area for the purpose of preserving specific species of animals or habitats is fine as far as it goes, but locking humans out of vast areas of the earth as if a human merely passing by is going to somehow despoil the perfection of nature is pagan worship of the creation rather than the Creator, and directly defies God's created order.

There are tonnes of examples of humans making the natural world better, including reclaiming deserts, spreading water via irrigation networks, and managing land to make it more diverse and productive.

Places like Europe have increasing amounts of forest despite the increasing population, thanks to oil and gas replacing wood as a primary energy source for heating in their cold winters. The world's farmed land area has been *decreasing* even as crop yields globally have been increasing, thanks to technology making farming more efficient and productive.

Via wealth and technology humans are becoming more *efficient* and as a result we are not a virus on the planet we depend on at all.

I do believe we should take steps to ensure animal species don't go extinct and that endangered habitats that cannot be easily replaced get preserved—that's all *part* of leaving an inheritance to our children's children and being good stewards of the earth that we've been given.

But we should *also* be mining resources, creating new technologies, exploring, building bridges and power stations and faster aeroplanes and more advanced computers, and doing everything in our power to make the best possible *use* of the resources we've been given, *also* for the sake of the inheritance we leave to our children's children.

Both the preserving *and* the creating are in obedience to God's instruction to fill and subdue the earth and His admonition to leave an inheritance to our children's children.

Consider the parable of the Talents which Jesus tells in Matthew 25. A master goes on a long journey and entrusts three servants with three different amounts of 'talents,' which were a unit of money but also appropriately refer to the natural gifts and abilities which God entrusts to each of us.

One servant was given five talents, and he invested those and ended up with ten. The master was happy with him. Another servant was given two talents and he invested those and ended up with four and the master was also happy with him. One servant was given just a single talent. He was afraid to invest it, for fear of losing it, and so he buried it. When the master returned he was angry, *not* that this servant didn't have ten talents, or four talents, but that he had not made use of the single talent he had been given.

God is not unreasonable. He knows that if you have only one talent to begin with then you cannot be expected to provide the same returns as someone with five talents, but He does insist that you use what you *have* been given to the best of your ability to provide a return.

The earth has been *given* to us, yes to steward, but also to *use*, to create a return and pass that return on to our children and grandchildren. To refuse to use those resources, to leave the metals or oils in the ground, the technologies unknown, the depths of the ocean or the vastness of space unexplored, is to bury the talents and resources that we've been given and from which God expects us to generate a return.

These two world views, the God-given pro-human world view and the Satanic anti-human pagan world view, are completely incompatible. Either God is true, or God is not. And if God is the Creator, the designer of the universe we inhabit, then His every word is true and Satan is a liar.

Satan's lies only serve to steal, kill, and destroy, and It's no coincidence that the epidemic of mental illness and youth suicide has come along with the rejection of God and the rise of anti-human humanism.

And it's refreshingly great news to know that God is pro-human and has given us all things richly to enjoy, including the resources here on God's green earth, and it is our privilege, our responsibility, and indeed our *joy* to get to make use of everything we've been given. We get to *subdue* the earth for the glory of God and for the purpose of leaving an inheritance to our children's children in accordance with God's word.

That *is* great news for all who will accept the challenge and responsibility of living and stewarding the earth in accordance with *God's* design rather than man's... but the bad news is, we live in a culture, nationally and globally, that has swallowed the lies of Satan hook, line, and sinker.

We see this in many ways, but none more obvious than the impending population collapse.

The human population is peaking now. Like, in your lifetime.

If current trends continue the human population will be in solid decline by 2050. And that's not a good thing.

It's obvious that population can't increase forever, but the mistake that *The Population Bomb* and *Limits to Growth* made is that they assumed the population would increase until resources ran out. That's not how God designed us.

What demographers have long known is that as humans get wealthier they have fewer children. Yep, weirdly, as resources and wealth *increase*, our population growth *decreases.* This has been true for thousands of years and appears to be a part of

God's design for us, presumably as a natural mechanism to ensure we would never over-populate the earth.

This 'population paradox,' of being wealthier leading to fewer children, was true in ancient Greece and ancient Rome, where the poor masses and the far-flung barbarians consistently out-bred the wealthy aristocracy.

It was true in ancient Egypt when the Hebrews outbred the richer and more powerful Egyptian natives until the Egyptians enslaved the Hebrews out of fear of their numbers!

This has *always* been true across time and across cultures, and it's still true today. For some reason wealth equals a lower average birth rate. So as the world has become wealthier the reproduction rate has declined and we've been able to calculate what the likely peak of human population would be if we just let nature run its course.

The assumption was that this peak would be reached rather gently and then the population would stabilise and hover around that number—projected to be about 11 billion people on or around the year 2100.

For some time it's been understood that the human population would naturally reach about that level by about that time and that no interventions would be needed to 'cap' the human population. The natural effect of us becoming wealthier would cause population growth to slow to a stop naturally and peacefully.

But that's not what's happening.

To keep the population stable each couple would need to give birth to approximately 2.1 children. 2 children to replace the 2 adults involved, and an extra .1 to allow for those who die without then creating children of their own. This is known as the 'replacement rate.'

But birth rates in wealthy countries have not dropped to replacement rates and stabilised as demographers assumed they would... they've collapsed *through* replacement rates and continued falling!

An anti-human world view has spread, leading some people to be selfish and not 'want' children, others to believe the world is ending due to climate change so they don't want to bring children into it, others to believe the earth is over-populated so they're not having children so as to not 'add to the problem'... the particulars vary, but they're all different expressions of Satan's anti-human world view.

As I write this there is almost no advanced economy on earth which is having enough children to replace their own population, and in most advanced economies the population is increasing *only* due to immigration.

That immigration is coming from less advanced and less prosperous countries where the birth rates are, for the moment, still above replacement rate, but that's changing.

As Africa and Asia emerge out of poverty and into some level of basic wealth with food security, basic medical care, and education, birth rates are falling fast.

And based on what's happening in wealthier and more advanced economies, there's no reason to expect their birth rates to stabilise once they get down to replacement rates. As these poor countries rapidly become wealthier over the next few decades they too will no longer be having enough children to sustain their own population, much less keep losing people to outward migration.

Which means that within probably 30 years even the countries where the population is growing will go into decline. At that point there will be no 'surplus' of people for wealthy countries to import through immigration, and global human population will go into reverse, fast.

This anti-human world view had already led to this trend being firmly established before the mRNA jabs came in to the picture, and what's happened since then has only accelerated the collapse.

There's rapidly mounting evidence that the mRNA jabs pushed on the world during Covid have had a negative effect on fertility and infant mortality, and have given rise to the Sudden Adult Death Syndrome, or 'SADS' phenomenon, especially among young, fit males.

Look at the work of Dr Naomi Wolf and her analysis of the Pfizer papers if you'd like to know more about that. You may recall that the Pfizer papers are the testing and safety documents that Pfizer tried to keep hidden for seventy years but were forced by a US Court to release.

Pfizer responded by releasing hundreds of thousands of pages of documents, presumably hoping that the truth would be buried in the sheer volume of information, but they didn't count on Dr Wolf putting together a taskforce to systematically examine every single page and summarise the evidence in plain English for the public to understand.

You can search online for her work or read her book *The Pfizer Papers: Crimes Against Humanity*.

When I interviewed Dr Wolf in 2023 I was shocked at her insistence that the devastating effect of mRNA jabs on fertility was intentional and not merely a horrific mistake, and I challenged her to explain her conclusion.

By default I tend to use 'Hanlon's Razor,' which says, "Never attribute to malice that which is adequately explained by stupidity."

I can accept the evidence showing the damage the mRNA jabs have caused, without necessarily believing it was intentional. By default, I'll assume it was stupidity, or greed, laziness, or some other human failing, before I'll believe that it might have been on purpose, so I asked Dr Wolf to explain why she had concluded it was intentional.

Dr Wolf pushed back in no uncertain terms, pointing out that the majority of the pre-release testing of the mRNA jabs in rodents was focused on fertility and clearly showed damage to fertility, yet that damage did not delay the release of the mRNA jabs! It was known and observed... but didn't seem to be a concern. Further, compared to the amount of testing and reporting on fertility, there was relatively little testing or reporting on the effectiveness of the jabs against a respiratory virus, which is what we were being told these jabs were for!

It boiled down to this question: If it *was* about reducing human fertility, what would they have done differently?

The answer is, 'nothing.'

They made a jab which reduced fertility, they tested and reported on its effect on fertility, and then, knowing it would devastate human fertility, they released it to the public and lied that it was 'safe and effective.'

That's the conclusion Dr Wolf shared with me based on what she found in the Pfizer Papers, and you can read her reports online or buy her book which lays it all out in detail for your own consideration.

Billions of people were bullied or terrorised into taking an experimental jab which didn't stop transmission of Covid, didn't stop hospitalisation or death from Covid, but did (and was known to) reduce human fertility. To cap it all off, the effects of the jabs on fertility and life expectancy are being blamed on 'Long Covid' by politicians and media.

It's the perfect crime with the perfect cover, and the drug companies made billions of dollars committing these anti-human crimes against humanity!

Sound like a conspiracy theory? I agree, it does.

But the more time passes the more evidence is stacking up to suggest it's the truth, and it's getting harder and harder to pass it off as a mistake, or as stupidity.

Regardless of your opinion on the mRNA jabs, what's certain is that the decline in birth rates is accelerating faster than demographers expected, meaning human population will peak well before the year 2100, and that reproduction rates will collapse below replacement rate and cause a collapse in the global human population.

Earth's population will never get to 11 billion people. Probably not to 10 billion in 2050 as used to be predicted, and possibly not even to 9 billion, despite being at 8.2 billion as I write this.

Birth rates are collapsing *that* fast, and unless there is a massive cultural shift world-wide, a rediscovering of God's pro-human plan for our planet, leading to a new baby boom, population collapse is all but inevitable.

Those Georgia Guide Stones calling for a population of 500,000,000 human beings? That sounded impossible when they were erected in 1980, but could be reality far sooner than you might think, and we'll likely be most of the way there within my children's lifetime.

Those Malthusians who argued that humans were a virus, and the Eugenicists who insisted we needed to reduce the population *and* 'direct' reproduction to create a world with a smaller, *better* population of humans... what if they aren't a relic from the 1800s and 1900s? What if their ideas are alive and well, and some powerful Malthusians and Eugenicists figured out a way to make their vision for mankind a reality?

What if this is simply the continuation of the age-old struggle between good and evil, between God's design for mankind to 'fill and subdue' and Satan's counterfeit to 'reduce and rewild'?

What if, despite all our technology, culture, and 'advancement,' humans are still just pawns in a cosmic battle between good and evil? What if the veneer we built, the supposed intelligence and sophistication of 'modern' humans, was just a façade, and the spiritual war has raged on unabated behind the scenes all this time?

What if this is Romans 1:20—"Professing themselves to be wise they became fools"?

And what if we need to wake up to the fact that we are in a spiritual war-zone, fast?

John Eldredge, the author of Wild at Heart, says it well: "Life is a love story set in a world at war."

The love story is the story of God's undying love for all of His children, His sons and daughters who have been separated from Him by sin and whom He longs to be reunited with, which is why He sent His Son, Jesus Christ, to pay the price of sin and make a way of reconciliation.

Against that love there stands the enemy, Satan, the fallen angel who can never be forgiven because there is no way of salvation for angels, only for mankind, and he's determined to take as many of God's human sons and daughters with him to eternal damnation as he can.

And that's what makes the earth a war zone. It's a perpetual war between good and evil as they battle over our human souls, and this war has been raging for *all* of human history and will continue until God ends the war in a final victorious battle.

But God is gracious and patient, and is allowing as much time as possible for people to repent of their sin and be reconciled to Him before He returns in power and victory, defeats Satan, and brings about the great and terrible judgement day.

God is pro-human. Humanity is the jewel of His creation; all creation was made *for* mankind, and mankind was given authority *over* creation.

Satan is anti-human. Humanity is the focus of all his hatred and he is working to counterfeit the created order and cause mankind to worship the *creation* rather than the Creator.

What if large sections of the Church have fallen for the counterfeit?

What Would Jesus Do?

There is one very important voice we have not heard from yet regarding Christians and civil disobedience, and it's the voice of our Lord and Saviour, Jesus Christ Himself.

When we ask ourselves the question, "What would Jesus do?" we have to keep in mind that whipping people and flipping tables is *within the realm of possibility*, because that's exactly what He did to the money-changers in the temple, as is recorded in John 2.

Now, I'm not suggesting that whipping people and flipping tables should be our go-to response! That was something Jesus did once, and specifically against the high-and-mighty religious and financial leaders and institutions of His day!

Jesus always responded with phenomenal grace and kindness to the poor, the needy, sinners, and broken people. His righteous anger was reserved for the religious and political leaders of the day.

But that does beg the question... if Jesus were alive today and saw the idolatry of the Church at an institutional level, the way that churches have partnered with government for money and power... how would He respond?

Hold that thought for a moment and let's back up. We're going to examine the story of the 'tribute coin' and the events that led up to Jesus saying, *"Render unto Caesar* [the government] *that which is Caesar's, and unto God that which is God's,"* because this is a pivotal moment in Jesus' ministry and is important for understanding the relationship between God and government. We're going to take a close look at that event soon, but to fully understand what is happening in that moment we need to understand more of what was going on in that time in history.

Answering questions with questions was a standard debating technique and the ultimate aim when rabbi (Jewish teachers) debated each other was to ask a question which the other rabbi did not want to answer at all, either with a 'yes' or a 'no.'

Essentially, the idea was to trap your opponent into a no-win situation. We see the Pharisees try to do this to Jesus repeatedly, and every time He responds with divine wisdom and astounds the Pharisees.

Consider the example of the woman caught in adultery:

The teachers of the law and the Pharisees brought a woman who had been caught in adultery. They forced her to stand before the people. They said to Jesus, "Teacher, this woman was caught having sexual relations with a man who is not her husband. The law of Moses commands that we stone to death every woman who does this. What do you say we should do?" They were asking this to trick Jesus so that they could have some charge against him.

But Jesus bent over and started writing on the ground with his finger. When they continued to ask Jesus their question, he raised up and said, "Anyone here who has never sinned can throw the first stone at her." Then Jesus bent over again and wrote on the ground.

Those who heard Jesus began to leave one by one, first the older men and then the others. Jesus was left there alone with the woman standing before him. Jesus raised up again and asked her, "Woman, where are they? Has no one judged you guilty?"

She answered, "No one, sir."

Then Jesus said, "I also don't judge you guilty. You may go now, but don't sin anymore."

— John 8:3-11

Notice that they asked Jesus about this woman specifically to have 'some charge against Him' and be able to accuse Him.

As a rabbi, Jesus had to uphold the law of Moses, so He couldn't say to let her go—if He did let her go then the Pharisees would accuse Jesus to the Jewish people for breaking the Law of Moses. But if Jesus *did* condemn the woman to death, as per the law of Moses, then He would be breaking Roman law which banned the death penalty for religious offences, and the Pharisees could have denounced Jesus to the Romans.

It was a win-win question for them and I'm sure the Pharisees felt very clever as they threw the woman to the ground in front of Jesus, certain that one way or the other they were going to destroy Jesus then and there.

All the Pharisees needed was an answer—*any* answer! But Jesus said, "Let the sinless man cast the first stone," and wrote on the ground with His finger. We don't know what He wrote, but it would make sense for Him to be writing the Ten Commandments... can you imagine standing there with a stone in your hand watching the commandment 'thou shalt not lie' being written in the dirt as you contemplate killing a woman for breaking the commandment 'thou shalt not commit adultery'?

I think it's telling that it was the older men who dropped their stones first. I think that's perspective and life experience at work. The younger hot-heads were more willing to go through with it despite their own guiltiness, but the older and wiser men understood their culpability and walked away first.

I can tell you from personal experience that I've mellowed enormously over my few decades of life, and where I would once have been among the hot-heads, I'd like to believe that today I'd be among the men who walked away first, or perhaps even among those who never picked up a stone in the first place.

Notice that after a short while Jesus and the woman were left completely alone. That means even the Pharisees left.

This is important.

What we know from this is that the Pharisees couldn't even keep asking their question after Jesus had given them that answer. For a Pharisee to continue to stand there, stone in hand, would be to claim to be sinless, which is blasphemy.

The question which the Pharisees had intended to be a win-win for them had turned into a total loss, a question they could not so much as *ask* again or it would be heresy. This is important to note, because this is how Jesus would always answer them when they tried to trap him.

This is how it works, and this is important to know as we consider the example of Jesus with the tribute coin.

It's important to know that at the time of Jesus there was a tax revolt underway, a violent affair led by a man named Judas of Galilee (no, not Judas Iscariot who betrayed Jesus, a different guy) and it was so intense that it had led to a few pitched battles, some fires, and quite a few deaths, including the deaths of both of Judas of Galilee's sons.

Passion was high and this 'tribute' tax, payable by Jews to the Romans, was a point of life-and-death conflict. People on both sides were willing to kill over it.

This made it the perfect subject for a win-win question for the Pharisees to ask Jesus:

Then they sent to Him some of the Pharisees and the Herodians, to catch Him in His words. When they had come, they said to Him, "Teacher, we know that You are true, and care about no one; for You do not regard the person of men, but teach the way of God in truth. Is it lawful to pay taxes to Caesar, or not? Shall we pay, or shall we not pay?"

But He, knowing their hypocrisy, said to them, "Why do you test Me? Bring Me a denarius that I may see it." So they brought it. And He said to them, "Whose image and inscription is this?" They said to Him, "Caesar's."

And Jesus answered and said to them, "Render to Caesar the things that are Caesar's, and to God the things that are God's."

And they marvelled at Him and left Him and went their way.

— Mark 12:13-17

There's a lot in that passage, so let's break it down.

Firstly, the stakes could not be higher. This is a literal life-or-death moment for Jesus. If He says it *is* lawful to pay taxes to the Romans then the tax rebels will have him dead within the week. If He says it's *not* lawful then the Romans will have him dead before dark.

The Pharisees had worked hard on their win-win question and they thought they'd got Him.

But they had underestimated the wisdom of Jesus Christ the Son of God.

Notice that the coin Jesus requested was not any old coin, but specifically the denarius that was required as the tribute. A Roman coin for a Roman tax.

Naturally, the Pharisees had some Roman coins handy... they did business with the Romans all the time!

This was a time when many coins from many kingdoms were in circulation, and you had to use Jewish currency in the temple, Roman currency for your taxes, etc. This is why the temple money changers had become so rich, and also why Jesus had become so cross with them back in John 2.

The Roman denarius in circulation at that time was the coin of Julius Tiberius Caesar. It had an image of Tiberius Caesar, of course, but Jesus also draws attention to the 'inscription' or the words on the coin. There must be something significant in those words specifically.

What did the inscription on that coin say? We know what it said because we've found many of them in archaeological digs. The inscription said:

"Caesar Augustus Tiberius, Son of the Divine Augustus."

Jesus drew everyone's attention to the fact that here on this coin Tiberius was claiming to be the *son of a god.*

Do not think that this was an accident. Consider how precisely Jesus has dealt with the other traps which the Pharisees have laid for Him. His choice to ask for that coin by name, and to draw attention to the words, was 100% intentional, and Jesus knew exactly what He was doing.

It is no accident that the actual Son of God held up exactly the coin on which Caesar claimed to be the son of god, and then told the Pharisees "Render unto Caesar that which is Caesars, and unto God that which is God's."

The perfection of this reply can be seen in the Pharisees' response: They marvelled, and then they left.

They did not even re-ask the question! They couldn't! In the same way that the Pharisees who accused the woman of adultery could not stay there with stones in hand or else they would be claiming to be sinless and therefore committing blasphemy, these Pharisees could not press their attack by re-asking the question or they would be suggesting that maybe Tiberius' claim to be the son of a god could actually be valid!

Jesus completely trapped them and, as He did so often, turned their question into a trap for the askers.

If you doubt that this is true please find another reason why they wouldn't have pressed the question? They *couldn't lose*, or so they thought—it didn't matter which *way* Jesus answered, it mattered only *that* He answered!

So why not keep asking?

They could have said "Yes, yes, Jesus, that's very cute, but really, is it lawful to pay the tax or not?"

That would have seemed like a completely reasonable answer if *not* for the fact that the very question itself was now toxic! It couldn't be asked again! To do so would mean the Pharisees were themselves open to calling Tiberius Caesar the son of god, which would be a blasphemy punishable by death.

Many preachers today say that Jesus' reply meant that we should pay taxes, but if that were really his reply then the Pharisee's response would make no sense at all.

The Bible does tell us to pay taxes (even though it was not part of God's design), but that's not what happened in this passage. The Pharisee's marvelled and ceased their attack precisely because that's *not* what Jesus said.

Jesus turned their question about tax into a question about who had a legitimate claim to be the Son of God, and in effect His statement, "Render unto Caesar that which is Caesar's, and render unto God that which is God's," is reminiscent of the challenge that Joshua gave to the Israelites as they finished conquering the Promised Land and were about to go to their homes: "Choose you this day whom you will serve."

Joshua gave that ultimatum in Joshua 24:15, and you'll recall that's how I started this book.

That was no accident.

That challenge, that ultimatum to 'choose whom you will serve,' is quite literally the ultimatum that is upon all of our lives from the moment we are born till the moment we die.

It is the only choice that matters.

When Jesus said "render under Caesar that which is Caesar's, and to God that which is God's," He was making a challenge.

"If you believe Tiberius' (or the government's) claim to be the son of god, then give him what belongs to him. But be sure to give to the one true God what belongs to Him."

He stood before them as the true Son of God, holding up the image of the false son of god who was the most powerful man on earth, the idol of government in human form, and He said, "God or government? Whom will you serve?"

A Bowl of Stew

Esau and Jacob were the fraternal twins of Isaac, son of Abraham—yes, the Abraham who received great promises from God that out of him would come a great nation.

But Abraham himself only had one son to his wife Sarah, which was Isaac, and Isaac had two sons, the twins Esau and Jacob.. Abraham did also have another son to his servant Hagar, whose name was Ishmael and although Ishmael was not the child that God promised and was therefore not the inheritor of 'the' promise, he still inherited the blessing that was on Abraham and his descendants are still with us to this day, proving that God is faithful even when we aren't... but that's an aside.

Back to Isaac and his twin sons Esau and Jacob.

Esau was the elder and therefore had the 'birthright' as the eldest son. By modern standards, the idea of a 'birthright' for the eldest son seems deeply unfair, but for whatever reason it was considered obvious 'back in the day' and was widely practised across many cultures in ancient times.

The firstborn son would typically receive a double portion of the inheritance, among other perks, and the 'firstborn' rule applied even to the elder of two twins, when the eldest was older by literally just minutes.

So Esau had it all: he was the firstborn son of the only legitimate son of the man whom God had promised to make a great nation from. Life was going to be great!

Esau was also loved by his father Isaac because he was a skilful hunter and his dad loved to eat meat! But Jacob, the younger, was content to stay at home "among the tents," according to the account in Genesis 25.

However, all was not as it seemed. Their mother Rebekah had felt them fighting when they were in the womb and when she prayed and asked God what was going on, God replied, in Genesis 25:23, *"Two nations are in your womb, and two peoples from within you will be separated; one people will be stronger than the other, and the older will serve the younger."*

So Jacob, the younger, was a mummy's boy, smooth skinned and happiest in the tents, while Esau was his fathers favourite, a man's man, ruddy, hairy, a hunter, and the inheritor of the birthright.

Until one day everything changed, just as God had said.

Once when Jacob was cooking some stew, Esau came in from the open country, famished. He said to Jacob, "Quick, let me have some of that red stew! I'm famished!"

Jacob replied, "First sell me your birthright."

"Look, I am about to die," Esau said. "What good is the birthright to me?"

But Jacob said, "Swear to me first." So he swore an oath to him, selling his birthright to Jacob.

Then Jacob gave Esau some bread and some lentil stew. He ate and drank, and then got up and left.

So Esau despised his birthright."

— Genesis 25:29-34

It's a weird passage, I'm not gonna sugarcoat it! Esau comes home so hungry that he's convinced himself he's going to die if he doesn't eat right now? Like... he can't wait till dinner? Or grab a snack of his own? Or cook up what he came home with from the hunt?

I get that there were no drive-through McDonald's and the nearest Chinese takeaway was... in China... but even so, this seems like a deeply emotional need for food rather than a truly physical one. If you're going to die from lack of food before dinnertime I don't think you're having a conversation about it with your little brother! I don't think you'd be moving or speaking at all!

But Esau became so convinced that his 'need' for food was life-or-death that he despised his birthright. He gave away his God-given birthright (it was God who decided who came out first!) in return for a bowl of stew.

I hope it was really good stew!

It would be tempting to believe that we wouldn't be that stupid, that we would never give away something so valuable as a birthright in return for a single meal, but history proves that humans do it all the time, and you and I are not immune. Time and again throughout history we get convinced that it's more than just a meal... it's more than just being really really hungry... it's life or death!

When it isn't.

Our fear makes us desperate for safety but in return for being protected, saved, or provided for in this 'life or death' situation, we despise our birthright and give up the blessings and freedoms that God intended for us. And all we get in return is a bowl of stew.

I mentioned already the Hegelian Dialectic of 'Problem, Reaction, Solution,' and how powerful people like to use it to manipulate the masses into demanding the very thing those powerful people wanted to do in the first place.

Proverbs 28:1 has a slightly different take on the idea: "The wicked flee when no one pursues, but the righteous are bold as a lion."

The wicked flee when no one pursues? Why would anyone do that? Because they believe a situation to be life-or-death when really it isn't. Because they fall prey to the Hegelian Dialectic and react in the manner they've been manipulated to react in rather than in a way that makes sense. They flee because they're Esau and they despise all that is greatest about God's gifts to us and trade it in for a little temporary sustenance to 'save' them from an imaginary death.

But we wouldn't do that right? Not us, not modern, enlightened man?

I think you already know the answer.

The most obvious recent example is Covid. People fled into their homes, they fled to their government for help, and when the government told them to flee from their churches they unquestioningly complied.

Families said goodbye to loved ones dying of non-Covid causes via Zoom or through windows, for fear of this unremarkable Coronavirus, and more crucially, around the world people abandoned their God-given rights to property, freedom, family, and worship, and handed total power to governments.

We gave up our birthright, our God-given freedoms and rights, for a little temporary safety... a bowl of stew.

In the same way that Esau convinced himself he wasn't going to live till dinner time, we convinced ourselves that this virus was a 'once in a hundred year' threat to us all... so what good is our God-given freedom, our God-given private property, our God-mandated work and the inheritance we're supposed to leave to our children's children, or our God-given mandate to gather together to worship and obey Him... what good is any of that if we're all dying from a virus?

That's absurd, of course. We knew by March 2020 that this virus was not a 'threat to us all' but facts didn't matter—just as Esau didn't care that, given he was able to walk and talk, he was not about to perish that day from a lack of food.

There was nothing pursuing us, but we fled anyway. And more tellingly, we fled not to God, but to the government.

Compare this to the actions of faithful men and women of God throughout Church history who have, when the times have called for it, gone to the place of danger. Some Christian men have volunteered as medics or as chaplains in times of terrible war, and served faithfully at great personal peril and in some cases at the cost of their lives.

At other times in history monks, nuns, and Christians of all denominations have given up cosy lives in the Western world to travel to far-flung places and minister specifically to the poor, the needy, and the diseased.

They went looking for those who were losing their mortal lives and brought them the gift of eternal life.

They did what the Church ought to have done in Covid—to have thrown our doors open wide as the media and political fear campaign ramped up, and called for all who would hear us to come in and repent of their sins for the judgement day of the Lord might be nearer than they think!

And what we most certainly should not have done is showed the same fear and idolatry as the world around us.

Consider the combined examples of Shadrach, Meshach, and Abednego, as well as the example of Daniel himself, whom I mentioned earlier in the chapter A Closed Door.

To recap Daniel, he continued to pray as he had done before. He did not show any fear or any obedience to the diktats of mankind.

As for Shadrach, Meshach, and Abednego, these three young men found themselves in positions of favour. The government liked them and their influence was increasing despite being captives in the land.

This is much like many churches and denominations today who have managed to obtain a position of favour with government, with influence, connections, mutual support, and money flowing relatively freely from the government into these churches.

When you find yourself in such a situation it's easy to rationalise not rocking the boat, not 'throwing away' the position that 'God has given' you.

I've heard pastors in private conversation try to explain to me the importance of them, their church, and their denomination 'staying on the good side' of the government for practical reasons. Often these 'reasons' come down to money and power, but not always. I accept that many of these pastors are sincere in their faith and serious in their calculus of how much good they are doing in their various charities and how much good they would be giving up if they upset the government and lost the funding, the support, the connections.

But what they miss is what they're giving up by selling their birthright for a bowl of stew, giving up obedience to the One True God for an idol of government, trading the truth of God for the counterfeit of Satan.

The Church is the bride of Christ, the bearer of the good news of the Gospel, the custodians of the keys to eternal life, and it is our responsibility, our privilege, and our joy to be a shining light that shines all the more in darkness.

The Church is not, first and foremost, a charitable organisation. Yes, we are called to do good works including charitable work for the poor, oppressed, and unfortunate. That's absolutely a part of what we're called to do as believers individually and as a church together.

But that's an outworking of our faith, one of its fruits. We are to demonstrate our faith by our good works, not do good works in place of having faith.

Our primary mandate is to go into all the world and preach the gospel, to make disciples, and to provide a gathering place for believers to encourage each other and keep our faith burning bright.

Charity is great! "Faith without works is dead," as James says, but works without faith is a pathway to Hell.

What this means in practice is that we should never compromise our beliefs for our works! If the government threatens our charitable programs unless we bow to them, we must uphold our faith and faithfulness to God uncompromised and let everything else go.

In my last book, Good People Break Bad Laws, I gave the example of a police officer who was caught on video having a verbal altercation with a protester during the Covid lockdowns in Melbourne. I'll recount the incident here, with apologies to those who have already read Good People Break Bad Laws, because the lesson is directly applicable to the Church as well.

Keep in mind as you read this that this tense standoff happened during the height of the police violence against anti-lockdown protesters. This was a time when arrests were common, pepper spray and tear gas were tossed around like candy on Halloween, and police had a free pass to assault anyone they pleased and get away with it.

This showdown was caught on video by a protester:

Officer 1 [armed with an automatic rifle]: "Go home, otherwise they start issuing tickets. We don't wanna do it, but we will."

Protester: "If you don't want to do it, don't do it! Stand up for what you believe in rather than [indistinguishable]."

Officer 2: "Just go home, we get paid to do this, I'm just as over these lockdowns as you are, but unfortunately I gotta do what I gotta do."

Protester: "You don't have to do that, you don't have to do that, you're choosing to do that for a paycheque."

Officer 2: "I'm not skilled to do anything else mate, so unfortunately at this time in my life, that's what I have to do."

Protester: "Hey, and the people of us that aren't skilled? We don't get paid; we're not getting food at the moment."

Officer 2: "I hear you mate, my wife's in the same position, she's out of a job at the moment as well. I understand you being pissed off about it..."

The point I made in Good People Break Bad Laws and will reiterate here is that these officers knew in their conscience that their actions were wrong, but their responsibilities to their families had been weaponised against them and they were in a terrible bind. They had to choose between doing what was right for their conscience, or putting food on the table for their kids.

Notice that it's their desire to provide for their family and do the *right thing* for their wives and children that was now causing them to violate their consciences.

The Church faced the same dilemma.

I would argue that churches should not accept government funding for any charitable work for exactly this reason, but I'm an outlier in that view.

The reality is that most churches receive government funding or support in some form or other, mostly for 'charitable' purposes, and that means that pastors and elders are placed in a similar bind when their conscience requires them to disobey the government.

They can either do what their conscience requires, or keep providing for people in need via their government-funded charitable programs, not both.

You cannot serve God and mammon. You cannot serve God and an idol.

This is what Christ warned us against in Matthew 6:24: *"No one can serve two masters, either you will hate the one and love the other, or you will cling to one and despise the other. You cannot serve God and money."*

Ideally, you never make yourself dependent on government money in the first place—that's the most reliable way to avoid compromising in moments like this—but even that is difficult, because in Melbourne churches could be fined tens of thousands of dollars if they didn't obey the lockdowns, so there were still very real financial implications even if a pastor wasn't compromised by a dependence on government cash to fund charitable works.

Still, the situation is so much worse for any churches that accept government funding for charitable work, and we can hear echoes of those two police officers in the way pastors insisted they had to do as they were told or they'd lose the funding for their charitable work.

Where the officers said, "I need to feed my family," these pastors said, "We need to run the soccer academy," or "the food trucks," or "the youth programs," or "the homeless outreach ," or the... you get the idea.

They allowed the government to dictate how and when they could worship God in return for their welfare funding.

It's not that the charity is bad, but our works should never be prioritised above our faith and our obedience to God.

Our church charities, connections, and influence must never be made more important than the gospel we preach.

And I get it, it's so easy to rationalise a compromise. Ironically, we often use God as our excuse! "God gave us favour with the government and we shouldn't jeopardise what God is doing..."

This sounds holy, it makes us sound like we're putting God first, but God never calls us to compromise to 'protect' what He's doing; He calls us to be faithful to Him and to His word and leave the rest up to Him.

In a way this is another example of how the Church can take the name of the Lord in vain, invoking God's name as an excuse to compromise because of a misguided (but probably sincere) belief that they would be 'letting God down' or somehow damaging His work if they stood up for their faith and in the process damaged their relationships or funding.

When faced with such a choice we must be fearless and uncompromising like Daniel was, and like Shadrach, Meshach, and Abednego were too.

Shadrach, Meshach, and Abednego were ordered to worship King Nebuchadnezzar as a god. These three young men were sitting pretty with influence and power and respect, rising fast despite being captives. It would be incredibly easy and tempting to say, "Hey, God is doing an amazing work here and we really shouldn't jeopardise that by upsetting the king!"

It would have been so easy for them to look at the favour and grace God had given them and then use that very favour and grace as an excuse to compromise.

But this is idolatry—compromising our faithfulness to the one true God who has all the power in the universe, in order to 'protect our position' with a human power, a false god.

God doesn't need your help and He doesn't need you to 'protect' His work. He asks for your faith and your faithfulness.

It's not your job to 'protect' what you've been given, it's your job to be faithful to the Giver.

He will protect His gifts where He needs to, and as you please Him by faith and faithfulness you'll find He will give you greater and greater gifts to steward.

I often think that we really limit God by fearing to lose what He's given us, and in the process showing that we don't believe He has the power to protect, preserve, restore, and multiply His gifts to us.

As Job said after God allowed Satan to take everything away from him, "The Lord gives, and the Lord takes away, blessed be the name of the Lord."

This has to be our attitude towards even the gifts that are part of our ministry, the funding, connections, favour, congregation size, TV access, whatever. It's all given by God, and He never wants us to compromise just to protect those gifts from harm.

This was exactly the attitude of Shadrach, Meshach, and Abednego in Bible times. They were unafraid to 'lose' the position of influence, power, and respect they had in the court of King Nebuchadnezzar.

They recognised that their faithfulness to the Giver was more important than the gifts they'd been given, and willingly risked being burned alive in a flaming furnace instead of bowing to a false idol.

After these three men refused to bow down and worship, they were ratted out by some of their enemies in the kingdom:

"O king, there are some men of Judah whom you made officers in the area of Babylon that did not pay attention to your order. Their names are Shadrach, Meshach, and Abednego. They do not serve your gods and do not worship the gold statue you have set up."

Nebuchadnezzar became very angry and called for Shadrach, Meshach, and Abednego. When they were brought to the king, Nebuchadnezzar said, "Shadrach, Meshach, and Abednego, is it true that you do not serve my gods nor worship the gold statue I have set up? In a moment you will again hear the sound of the horns, flutes, lyres, zithers, harps, pipes, and all the other musical instruments. If you bow down and worship the statue I made, that will be good. But if you do not worship it, you will immediately be thrown into the blazing furnace. What god will be able to save you from my power then?"

Shadrach, Meshach, and Abednego answered the king, saying, "Nebuchadnezzar, we do not need to defend ourselves to you. If you throw us into the blazing furnace, the God we serve is able to save us from the furnace. He will save us from your power, O king. But even if God does not save us, we want you, O king, to know this: We will not serve your gods or worship the gold statue you have set up."

— Daniel 3:12-18

I believe these events are recorded in the Bible to teach us how to respond in exactly these kinds of situations!

Notice a few key points here. The accusers were careful to mention to Nebuchadnezzar that these three men had been 'made officers.' *I.e.*, they had the favour of the king. This was relevant in that situation because it made their disregard for the king's order 'even worse.' These weren't just peasants, these men were officers!

That promotion to a position of money and influence and power was supposed to bring obedience. Their status was supposed to give the king leverage over them.

It's the same when the government spends taxpayers' money on welfare programs via churches. The government fully expects that this 'favour' is going to be returned in the form of support and obedience from the Church.

Notice as well that Shadrach, Meshach, and Abednego did not feel the need to explain themselves or try and 'nuance' their way through the situation. In verse 16 they said,

"We do not need to defend ourselves to you."

They then make a combined statement of faith and of faithfulness.

The faith statement is, *"The God we serve is able to save us from the furnace,"* and is followed immediately by the statement of faithfulness: *"But even if God does not save us, we want you, O king, to know this: We will not serve your gods or worship the gold statue you have set up."*

They're not playing nice. They're not playing political games or hiding behind clever language. They're making their position crystal clear and they're not going to bow down, even if it costs them their favour with the government.

Once the government makes itself a false god, an idol, it must not be worshipped, no matter the cost—even if that 'cost' is the things that were gifts from God in the first place!

Daniel showed us that we must not even appear to obey the government over God, because just the appearance of obeying suggests compromise on our part. And Shadrach, Meshach, and Abednego show that we do not have to be apologetic about obeying our faith over government which has disobeyed its God-given purpose to reward good and punish evil; we must in fact be bold and make it absolutely clear that we praise and worship and serve the Giver of gifts, the one true God, and we will abandon the gifts themselves if keeping them would require us to bow down to idols.

God is gracious, patient, and forgiving, and all the pastors and believers and churches which compromised either through fear or for money or power, or even naïvely 'for the right reasons' can repent and be forgiven and fully restored.

But we need to get on with it.

I believe that far more severe tests of our faith are coming, within my lifetime, which will make the Covid era look like a mere warm up exam before the real thing. I believe that's exactly why God allowed Covid to happen as He did.

Every believer must examine our choices during Covid, the ways in which we were faithful to God and stood firm in the faith, and the ways in which we did not. The ways in which we conquered fear through faith and shone our light as brightly as possible... and the ways in which we hid our light through 'nuance' and 'Christian love.'

We must each of us repent where necessary, learn where possible, and steady ourselves against future temptations to compromise 'for the right reasons.'

Many believers as individuals, and many church denominations as institutions, failed the Covid test and ended up fleeing when no one was pursuing. They traded in their God-given birthright of faith, freedom, and liberty in Christ for a bowl of man-made stew in the form of false 'safety' and easy money. And they abandoned the fearless worship of the one true God for obedience to government, a man-made idol, all the while rationalising it as the 'Christian' thing to do.

It is up to each of us as believers to learn these lessons now, and to assist our churches and fellow believers to do the same, before another even greater test comes our way.

Obeying God in a Fallen World

The scariest thing that God can do to us is give us what we want. In fact in Scripture we often see that God judges people by giving them what they want!

So often we pray to God and then get mad because He just isn't giving us what we wanted, what we asked for, prayed for, fasted for…!

Why not? Doesn't He say to ask and we will receive? Doesn't He tell us to make our requests known to Him? Doesn't He say He delights in giving good gifts to His children?

Yes, He does say all of that. But the key to understanding what's happening is the phrase 'good gifts.' God delights in giving 'good' gifts, and most of the time if He gave us what we wanted it would not be 'good' for us. Not at all.

What if God knew that by allowing you to win the lottery you would go on to make a trainwreck of your life, destroy your marriage and your family, and end up in Hell?

Would it be a 'good' gift if He answered your prayers to win 'the big one' if that was the end result? Of course not.

It's obvious that, with God's eternal perspective in mind, nothing that leads to eternal damnation is a 'good gift.' So on the flipside, from God's eternal perspective, anything that leads someone to repentance and eternal life *is* a 'good gift,' no matter how much it hurts in the meantime.

Stop and think about that for a moment.

God in His goodness, kindness, and faithful love, will put you through hell on earth if it will save you from Hell in eternity.

And He will not give you a gift, not matter how 'good' you think it is, if He knows it will be your downfall to Hell. He loves you too much for that.

Satan is the one who tries to lead us astray with promises of riches, of an easy life, of power, of pleasure... and often he delivers on those promises in order to keep his victims in bondage and drag their souls to Hell.

God never wants that to happen, but Satan is crafty and people are very often deceived by Satan's lies, by his false promises, by the sin which is "sweet to the taste, but afterwards is as bitter as wormwood."

God loves those deceived people too, and wants to save them, so every now and then we see in Scripture that God 'gives people over' to what they want, which is to say, to what Satan has promised them, as a form of judgement here on this earth and as a last resort to give them a final chance at repentance.

Romans 1 which I quoted earlier in this book is just one of many examples in Scripture where God allows people to indulge in sin, debauchery, and depravity to the point that such people convince themselves there is no God, there is no one who sees them, and they will never face judgement for their actions.

Why does God do that when it leads always to such terrible evil, to sin and rebellion and suffering and pain here on earth?

Because He loves us enough to try to save our eternal souls, and sometimes as a last-resort He has to give us what we want so we can experience the pain and emptiness and soul-crushing bondage that comes from believing the lies of Satan.

God ‘gives us what we want’ in order to bring judgement upon us in this life, so that some of us will realise the lie, realise that we’ve been conned by Satan’s counterfeits, and will turn back to God before it is too late.

I believe that is exactly what is happening with the Church and our idolatry of government right now.

Like the children of Israel in the book of Samuel, who demanded a king to replace God, so the Church today is demanding the government do for us what God promised that He would do.

God promised to be our provider (Jehovah Jireh), but who do churches look to for funding today?

God promised to be our healer (Jehovah Rapha), but who did we look to for healing when Covid came?

It’s the same with all the other names of God. God declared Himself to be our giver of wisdom, our protector, our refuge and guide. Who does the Church look to for wisdom, guidance, protection, and refuge?

And just as God said to Samuel, “Listen to them and give them a king,” God is likewise giving us what we’re demanding.

You want the government to have the final say in every area of your life? Your finances, your health, your education, your faith? OK, here, have it.

But be careful what you wish for.

We are trading, in real time, the one true God for an idol, for a counterfeit of Satan which is destined to bring hell on earth. We are demanding that God give it to us... and the most terrifying thing is that God is giving us what we want.

There is a saying, "A government big enough to give you everything you want is a government big enough to take away everything that you have."

This quote is often misattributed to Thomas Jefferson, but there's no actual evidence he said it. It emerged in newspapers in the 1950s and was attributed to Jefferson for the first time (that we know of) in the 2000s.

But the origin of the quote is irrelevant, because it's entirely accurate regardless of who said it first.

A government that has the power to give you money has the power to take it. A government with the power to 'give' you your rights has the power to take them away. A government with the power to 'protect' your faith also has the power to attack it.

Time and again in history Christians have begged the government for 'help,' empowered the government to 'help,' and then discovered too late that they'd created a monster.

This can be seen as far back as the time of the Emperor Constantine, but I'll save you the history lesson and use a more recent example from when Christians in Australia made this mistake with the debate about the definition of marriage.

In December 2017 the Marriage Act was amended to remove reference to gender or sex, allowing any couple of any sex to marry under that law.

Many Christians lamented that the Church 'lost' the marriage debate in 2017.

But that's not true. The Church 'lost' the marriage debate in 1961 when the government passed the original Marriage Act in Australia and brought the sacred institution of marriage officially under the control of the secular civil government.

Or it could be argued that perhaps the Church 'lost' the marriage debate in Australia all the way back when the Australian Constitution was ratified in 1900 with section 51(21) giving the federal government the power to define and regulate marriage.

That was the moment when the sacred institution of marriage was placed into the realm of the profane and that which was created by God was placed under the control of man.

Of course at the time in 1900 there was no thought that the civil government would ever define marriage as being between anything other than a man and a woman, and it was believed that no real harm could come from giving government the authority to regulate such a crucial sacred institution as marriage.

But marriage wasn't created by government, it was created by God.

The Bible makes it clear that God's design is for marriage to be between a man and a woman. Scripture does allow the same man to have multiple wives but that's not God's ideal. God's *ideal* design for marriage given in 1 Timothy 3 is very clear: One man, one woman, for life.

This ideal design for marriage is so important that according to 1 Timothy you cannot hold a position of authority within the Church if you are married to more than one woman! So whilst polygamy was allowed by God, it was a disqualifier for holding any office in a church.

Marriage is a sacred institution and was already defined by God thousands of years ago.

But that wasn't good enough for us. We decided we needed the government to get involved. Just like the Israelites who weren't happy with God as their king, we decided that our civil government should have authority over the sacred institution of marriage.

The Australian Government was given power over marriage in 1900, but no definition of marriage was included in the constitution. It was not until 1961 that a federal 'Marriage Act' was passed, but still it did not actually define marriage, it just allowed for certain government documents and registers to provide 'services' to people who were getting married, and to keep records. This was so the government could help...

This is the trap.

Then in the late 1900s the argument over 'marriage equality' [sic] erupted and suddenly the definition of marriage was a battleground.

Prime Minister John Howard, a professing Christian, promised to 'help' us even more by adding a definition of marriage into the Marriage Act. Sounds like a good idea, right?

Except that what this does is assert that the definition of marriage is something that governments can change.

This was the final nail in the coffin for the sacredness of marriage, taking it fully out of the realm of the sacred and placing it entirely in the hands of profane man and his idolatrous government.

In 2004 John Howard added into the Marriage Act of 1961 a definition of marriage as the "union of a man and a woman to the exclusion of all others, voluntarily entered into for life."

Sounds great, right? Certainly many Christians celebrated this change in the naïve belief that marriage had now been 'protected' by the government, and indeed that's what Prime Minister Howard truly believed he was doing: he was helping.

I've met Mr Howard and he sincerely believes he was 'protecting' marriage. He absolutely feels his conscience is clear on this point.

But regardless of how he feels, in truth of this moment was a terrible defeat.

Because the Church celebrated the government defining marriage via legislation in 2004 it lost any moral authority to object when the government changed that definition fourteen years later.

Since then we've seen this issue weaponised via anti-discrimination laws, with many churches and many pastors allowing themselves to be bullied into participating in same-sex marriages for fear that if they don't they will be sued, or lose government funding, or some similar fate.

In short, it's just another example of the Church allowing the government to take the place of God, and when the government inevitably forces the Church to choose between them and God the temptation of government funding, Government-Jireh, is too strong and churches compromise on the God-given definition of marriage and instead adopt Satan's counterfeit of marriage in return for money and influence and social status in this fallen world.

Trading our birthright for a bowl of stew.

We've told God we don't need him because we have the government. Our churches have told God we don't need him. We've told God he's too legalistic, too 'fundamentalist,' not 'loving' enough... We've told God to take a back seat, because we know better and the government will take care of us.

We kicked God and His Ten Commandments out of the classroom, the courtroom, and the parliament, because the government told us not to be 'intolerant.'

We traded charity for welfare, gave up our God-given rights, changed the definition of marriage, and forgot what a 'woman' is, all because the government said, "We've got this."

We told God to go away.

What if God is saying, "OK"?

What if God is now giving us what we want—an idol, a false god, a modernised version of the 'king' that the Israelites demanded from Samuel?

And what if, in the process, we're returning to the idolatry of our ancient ancestors?

There's a wonderful book titled *Return of the Gods* by Jonathan Kahn, in which he argues that we are seeing an active, indeed an aggressive, return of the ancient spirits, the false gods that were worshipped by the Philistines, the Greeks, the Romans, and so many other cultures.

Principally these 'gods' are:

- Baal, the god of money and prosperity, whose sign is a bull and whose statue named 'charging bull' sits outside the famous Wall Street trading floor in New York city.

- Moloch, the god who demands human sacrifices, particularly children, and whose shrines can be found all over the Western world under the name 'family planning centre,' abortion clinics where children are sacrificed daily.

- Ishtar, the god of sensuality and sex, whose ancient annual festival in the month of Junium, which featured cross dressing, androgyny, and overt sexuality, has morphed into the modern day 'Pride' month of June.

I find Kahn's arguments persuasive, and I believe in all three cases these false gods have captured government and elevated it to the status of an idol, an object of human worship, and the means by which these spirits accomplish their goals on earth.

These three ancient but returned 'gods' are the animating force behind the rapid rise in the power and reach of government and explain the malice with which governments have come to target Christianity and Christians as they pass legislation in service of Baal, Moloch, and Ishtar.

I believe we have entered a moment in history when the veneer of 'civilisation' and technology is being stripped away, and the ancient war between good and evil, God and Satan, the Truth and the Lie, is being revealed once again to anyone with eyes to see and ears to hear.

Sadly, many Christians and churches have proved themselves unable, or perhaps more accurately, unwilling, to see or hear.

If you've read this far then hopefully you do have eyes to see and ears to hear and a heart that is willing to understand the battle in which we are engaged.

I believe there is only one way back from where we are.

The solution does not lie in politics, economics, sociology, or even demographics.

The solution, the only solution, lies in repentance.

We must renounce our idol of government and return to the worship of the one true God, and we must do it now.

Christians individually and churches as a body must publicly renounce the worship of and obedience to government, disentangle finances from government, and recommit ourselves to unashamed, unapologetic obedience to God and God alone.

As Daniel did when he prayed "as he did before" despite the law changing; as Esther did when she went to the king to petition for oppressed people, "Even though it is against the law;" as Moses did when he ordered Pharaoh to let the Israelites go against his wishes; as Jesus did when He said, "Render unto God that which is God's" in defiance of Tiberius' false claim to be the son of god; and as Joshua did when he said, "As for me and my house, we will serve the Lord," so must we do in our own lives, our own churches, and our own countries today.

And we must stand boldly by our faith, in compliance with our conscience, for the sake of 'doing good,' no matter the consequences.

As Esther did when she said, "If I die, I die;" as Shadrach, Meshach, and Abednego did when they said, "Even if our God doesn't save us, we will not bow down to you, O King;" as most of the apostles did when they went to their deaths for continuing to preach the gospel and build the Church in defiance of the civil authorities, we must be willing to pay whatever price for the sake of doing good, in accordance with our conscience, for the Lord's sake.

I do not know what the future holds, I do not know what challenges we will face, in what ways we will be tested, or in what ways your conscience will legitimately differ from mine.

All I know for certain is that you must obey your conscience before God, just as I must obey mine. We must each, with absolute sincerity, search out the truth of the gospel and the Bible and live by that as best we can regardless of what civil authorities may say.

And I know for certain that the time for compromise must come to an end, the idol of government must be rejected, and God and God alone must be worshipped.

It's time to choose.

Will You Obey God in this Fallen World?

Made in United States
North Haven, CT
03 November 2026

21729971R00143